P E R S O N A L   P R O D U C T I V I T Y   W I T H

dBASE III®

Kenneth D. Gorham
Los Angeles Mission College

wcb
Wm. C. Brown Publishers
Dubuque, Iowa

Copyright © 1987 by Wm. C. Brown Publishers. All rights reserved

Library of Congress Catalog Card Number: 87–70160

ISBN 0-697-05551-5

Printed in the United States of America
10 9 8 7 6 5 4 3 2 1

Contents

Preface

I have been involved in computer instruction for almost twenty years. In that time, I have watched computer use evolve from outdated, donated computers, through a period of extensive use of large, timeshared mainframes, to the current concentration on the microcomputer. Many colleges across the nation have purchased IBM PCs or compatible microcomputers. New classes were developed to teach the use of these microcomputers. At Los Angeles Mission College, I developed a course called Introduction to Microcomputer Applications. This course has a strong, hands-on emphasis. Since no textbooks existed to teach this material, I developed my own text.

This textbook, *Personal Productivity with dBASE III*®, is one of three textbooks that I have developed. The other two are *Personal Productivity with WordStar*® and *Personal Productivity with Lotus 1–2–3*®. The Introduction to Microcomputer Applications course teaches WordStar, Lotus 1–2–3, and dBASE III. The textbooks have been extensively tested for the last one and one-half years at Los Angeles Mission College. The texts have been proven successful in introducing students to the use of these application programs. As a consultant to many business and governmental organizations, I have found that these programs are used extensively by clerical and managerial personnel.

The three application programs, WordStar, Lotus 1-2-3, and dBASE III, have been chosen with care. These packages have consistently been the most widely used programs in their respective areas. They are also fine programs. I have used all of them extensively in my college and outside consulting work. I have found that they always have the power and flexibility necessary to meet any challenge.

The text assumes no prior knowledge on the part of the student. The tutorial exercises in these textbooks have been constructed to lead the student, step by step, through the most common uses of these software packages. Every step that the student must take is numbered. Every press of the ENTER key is indicated. I have found that you must not leave anything to the imagination when teaching this demanding material. The tutorials are constructed so that students may progress at their own pace. They may repeat any part of the tutorial as many times as is necessary to learn the material.

THE TUTORIAL LESSONS

Tutorial lesson 1 introduces the student to the dBASE III Assistant. The dBASE III Assistant is a menu-driven version of dBASE that became available when dBASE II was converted to dBASE III. The Assistant program introduces the student to the major dBASE III commands. The student can build a dBASE III command step by step by selecting portions of the command from a series of menus. The Assistant program displays a command line at the bottom of the screen, and the student can watch the command develop. A small database is developed in chapter 1. The student is then introduced to the Display command. Several types of Display commands are utilized.

The second tutorial lesson also utilizes the Assistant program to teach the basic dBASE III commands. The student appends a record to the database that was created in chapter 1. The Edit and the Browse commands are utilized to examine the contents of the database. The concepts of removing records from a database are introduced using the Delete, Recall, and Pack commands. Finally the student learns how to sort a database into a new sequence.

Chapter 3 introduces the student to the direct command mode of dBASE III. Using the knowledge that was built with the Assistant menus, the student learns how to use the Append, Display, Edit, Browse, Delete, Recall, and Pack commands at the dot prompt. In addition, several new commands are introduced. The Locate command is introduced, and two versions of the Locate command are utilized in the tutorial. The student learns how to find a record with the Locate command and then how to display that record with the Display command. The concept of indexing a database is introduced. The difference between the Index command and the Sort command is examined and explained.

In chapter 4 of the tutorial, the important concept of changing the structure of the database is introduced. The student uses the Modify Structure command to add two new fields to the database. The two new fields illustrate the Logical data type of field and the Date type of field. The three commands for numeric manipulation—Sum, Average, and Count—are introduced and explained. Finally the student utilizes the Modify Report and Report Form commands to create and print out reports from the database.

CHAPTER LEARNING AIDS

Numerous screen display checkpoints are included in each chapter. Students will be able to check their work against the screen displays to make sure that they have followed the steps correctly.

Each chapter begins with clear instructions on how to start up dBASE III and instructions on how to leave dBASE III when the tutorial is completed. The tutorial lessons may be repeated by the student as many times as necessary.

There are multiple-choice questions in a Mastery Quiz at the end of each chapter. In addition, discussion questions are included that require active recall of what students have learned. You will find that these discussion questions will provoke lively class discussions.

There is a keyboard diagram in chapter 1 that will introduce the student to the IBM PC keyboard. Each of the special control keys—ESC, TAB, CTRL, SHIFT, and ENTER—is labeled and discussed.

A dBASE III command summary is found at the end of the text. This command summary pinpoints the dBASE III commands introduced in this text.

A glossary of dBASE III terms is also found at the end of the text. Each of these terms was introduced in the four chapters of the text. The glossary provides a convenient summary of the important dBASE III terms.

HARDWARE

This text was designed for the IBM PC computer, with two disk drives and an Epson or IBM dot matrix printer. If you are using a PC compatible or an XT or equivalent, the materials could be easily adapted to these types of computers. Since the student creates all the database material used in the tutorial, these materials can be used without a special training disk.

ACKNOWLEDGMENTS

Mari Rettke of Los Angeles Mission College was involved from the beginning in the preparation and testing of these tutorial materials. Her suggestions and contributions were of the utmost importance in the production of this manuscript. Thanks to Nick Murray, developmental editor at Wm. C. Brown Publishers, for his many helpful suggestions and support.

I would like to thank the people who reviewed the manuscript for the helpful suggestions that contributed so much to its development: Joyce Abler, Central Michigan University; Carole Colaneri, Orange County Public Schools; Keith O'Dell, Olivet Nazarene University; and Eileen Wrigley, Community College of Allegheny County.

Mari Rettke and Kyla Goad of Los Angeles Mission College, provided the important checking and cross-checking of the tutorial instructions and accompanying screens. I would also like to thank the several hundred students in the Introduction to Computer Applications classes who were the test subjects for the earlier versions of this text.

1

Introduction to dBASE III

LEARNING OBJECTIVES

After completing chapter one the student will be able to:

1. Load DOS into RAM memory.
2. Load dBASE III into RAM memory.
3. Choose the ASSIST mode of dBASE III.
4. Create a database file using ASSIST.
5. Enter data into the database file
6. Use the Display command to display all of the database records.
7. Use the Display command to display only some of the fields within a database record.
8. Use the Display command to display only some of the records within a database file.
9. Use the ESC key to "back out of" a dBASE III command.
10. Use the F1 key to display a navagational menu that can be used to indicate where you are located within the ASSIST menu structure.
11. Leave the ASSIST mode and return to the dBASE III program.
12. Leave dBASE III and return to DOS.

dBASE III

dBASE III is a powerful database program. You have the ability to operate dBASE III in a menu-driven mode called *Assist,* or you may operate the program in a direct command-driven mode. The original dBASE program, which was called dBASE II, was famous for providing only the *dot prompt.* You brought the program up, were greeted with a single dot, and you had to know the commands to take the next step with the program. dBASE III is an improvement over dBASE II because it provides a menu-driven mode for beginners. Once you are experienced with dBASE III, you can move to the command-driven mode, which will allow you faster access to all the features of the program. dBASE II was the most popular database program on the IBM PC by a wide margin. dBASE III has continued to be the most popular database program on the IBM PC and it has recently replaced Lotus 1-2-3 as the most popular business application program on the IBM PC.

FIELDS AND RECORDS

A database file consists of *fields* and *records.* Fields are groups of consecutive characters that contain data on one item. In the sample file used in this text, three fields are started:

Cust_Num field	contains the number for each customer
Cust_Name field	contains the name of each customer
Amount field	contains the amount owed per customer

1

The sample file that is created in dBASE III begins with three records, one record for each of three customers. Each record contains the customer number, customer name, and amount owed. A group of fields makes up a record and a group of records makes up a *file*.

ASSIST

The dBASE III program is so large that you must first "boot" the computer using the DOS diskette and then insert the dBASE diskette and start dBASE. To start dBASE, you enter dbase and press the ENTER key. You are then greeted with the infamous dot prompt.

In chapters 1 and 2, you are going to work with dBASE III in the Assist mode. This will allow you to use the menus until you are more familiar with the dBASE commands. To enter Assist mode, key in assist and press RETURN. A menu of general Assist instructions is then displayed on the screen as illustrated in figure 1.1.

```
                         The dBASE III
                           Assistant

        Assist uses menus to bring you the power of dBASE III


    -----------------------------------------------------------------
       KEY                            FUNCTION
    -----------------------------------------------------------------
    Esc                      Exit from current operation
    Up arrow                 Move to previous menu
    Down arrow               Move to next menu
    Left arrow               Move one item to the left
    Right arrow              Move one item to the right
    Home                     Go to first menu
    End                      Go to right most item
    Option Letter            Executes option (Unless otherwise noted
                             option letter is first letter of option)
    -----------------------------------------------------------------


    Press DOWN ARROW (or ENTER) to CONTINUE, ESC to EXIT ASSIST
```

Figure 1.1. The dBASE III Assistant.

The *ESC key* allows you to escape from a dBASE III Assist operation. If you want to back out of an Assist menu item, press the ESC key.

The arrow keys are used to move about the Assist menus. The *DOWN ARROW key* will move you down one menu level, and the *UP ARROW key* will move you up one menu level.

Assistant Main Menu

Press the ENTER key to go into the Assist mode. The Assistant Main Menu illustrated in figure 1.2 is displayed on the screen.

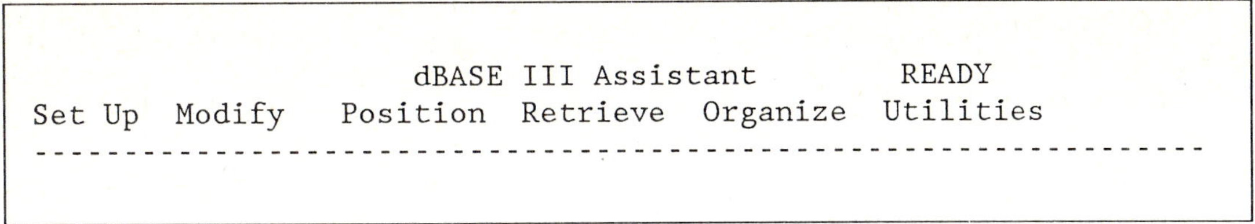

Figure 1.2. The dBASE III Assistant Main Menu.

The *menu cursor* highlights the *default menu choice* in each menu. The default menu choice is the first menu choice in each menu. To choose the default menu choice, press the ENTER key . To choose any other menu choice, you can use the arrow keys to move you to the menu item you want and then press the ENTER key. When you position the cursor on a menu item, dBASE III will display a help screen in the middle of your display that will give you a brief summary of the menu item that the cursor is on.

You can also choose a menu item by pressing the first letter of the menu item. You must be very careful with this technique. Some menus have several menu items that begin with the same letter. For example, the SET UP menu has as menu choices Create, Create Label and Create Report. If you entered "C" to choose a menu item, dBASE III would choose the first menu item that begins with a "C."

Set Up Environment Menu

Since you do not have a database to recall, your first action must be to create a database. Press the ENTER key to select the default menu choice of Set Up. The Set Up menu will be displayed as illustrated in figure 1.3.

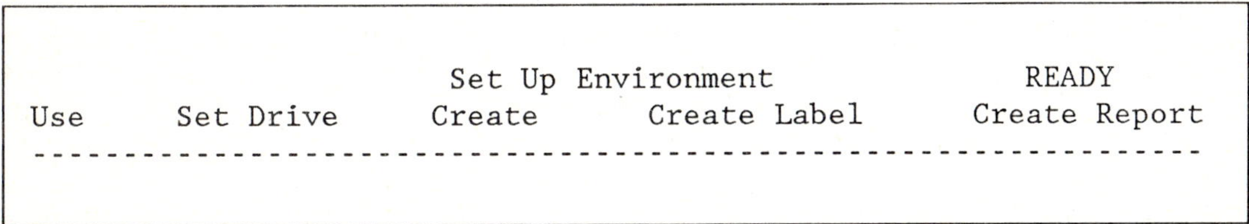

Figure 1.3. The Set Up Environment Menu.

Create Command

Select Create by pressing the RIGHT ARROW key twice and then pressing the ENTER key. The Create menu item allows you to set up a new database. You will then be presented with the Create a database screen displayed in figure 1.4.

```
                    Set Up Environment                    READY
    Use    Set Drive    Create      Create Label      Create Report
    -----------------------------------------------------------------
    Create a database    (C - Option letter)
    -----------------------------------------------------------------


    -----------------------------------------------------------------
    A filename  can consist of from 1 to 8 letters or digits.  A disk
    drive  letter  (A,B..)   and  a colon can precede  the  filename.
    Otherwise,  current disk drive is used.     Enter the name of the
    file: [          ]
    -----------------------------------------------------------------
    Command: Create
    No database is in use.

    Drive B: Previous menu: ↑ Left: ← Right: → Next: ↓ (or ENTER)
```

Figure 1.4. The Create Command Menu.

Name of File

Enter the name of the file as WIDGET and press the ENTER key. You will then be presented with the field creation screen displayed in figure 1.5.

```
    B:widget.dbf                              Bytes remaining:    4000
                                              Fields defined:        0


    -----------------------------------------------------------------
    : CURSOR   ←   →   :     INSERT    :     DELETE    :Up a field:    ↑ :
    : Char:   ←  →     : Char: Ins : Char:  Del :Down a field: ↓ :
    : Word: Home End : Field: ^N  : Word:  ^Y  :Exit/Save: ^End :
    : Pan:    ^←   ^→   :           :  Field: ^U :Abort:       Esc  :
    -----------------------------------------------------------------


     field name   type      width   dec  -----------------------------
       1 [        ]  Char/text [       ] [       ]



    Names start with a letter;  the remainder may be letters, digits,
    or underscore
```

Figure 1.5. Field Creation Screen.

Types of Fields

There are several different kinds of fields in dBASE III. You will create two character type fields and one numeric type field. Character fields can contain any character in the IBM PC character set. This means that you would be allowed to enter letters, numbers, and special characters into a character field. The customer name field is a perfect example of a field that could contain letters, numbers, or special characters.

Numeric fields are the only type of field that can be used in computations. Numeric fields can contain only numeric information (numbers, decimal points, and plus or minus signs). You will declare your amount field to be numeric so that this field can be used in computations.

You must give dBASE III three bits of information about your fields:

The name of the field
The field type (character or numeric)
The maximum width of the field and number of decimal positions if the field is a numeric field

After you have defined the three fields, press *control-end* (^END), which will end the field definition. Control-end will often be used to end a process in dBASE III. dBASE III will ask you to press RETURN (the ENTER key) to confirm that you have ended field definition. Press the ENTER key, and you will be presented with the prompt:

```
INPUT DATA RECORDS NOW? (Y/N)
```

dBASE III wants to know if you wish to enter data into your database file now or if you wish to enter data at a later date. You will press the Y key to answer "Yes." You will be presented with the input data screen illustrated in figure 1.6.

```
Record No.        1
------------------------------------------------------------------
: CURSOR    <--  -->  :           UP    DOWN :  DELETE     : Ins. Mode:Ins
:  Char:    <-   ->   :Field:     ↑     ↓    :Char:    Del : Exit:    ^End
:  Word:   Home End   :Page:     PgUp  PgDn  :Field:    ^Y : Abort:  Esc
:                     :                      :Record:  ^U : Text:   ^Home
------------------------------------------------------------------
CUST_NUM
CUST_NAME
AMOUNT
```

Figure 1.6. Input Data Screen.

Input Data

Now, enter data into your database. You have defined the structure of the database–field names, field types, and field width–but you have no data in your database. A data entry menu and a data entry screen will be provided by dBASE III to enable you to enter data. You will enter a customer number and press the ENTER key. You will enter a customer name and press the ENTER key. Finally, you will enter an amount and press the ENTER key. If you make a data entry error, consult the data entry menu to see which key will allow you to correct the error.

When you finish entering data, press ^END. You may exit a dBASE III operation by pressing ^END or by pressing ESC. Pressing ^END saves your work on disk and then exits the operation. Pressing ESC exits the operation, but does not save your work. Press the UP ARROW to move back up to the Assistant Main Menu displayed in figure 1.7.

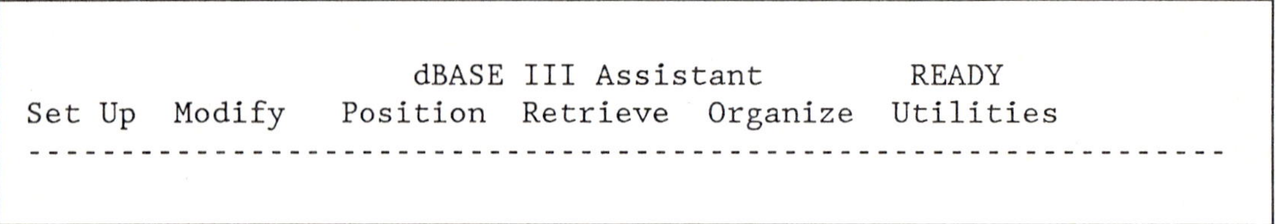

Figure 1.7. Assistant Main Menu.

Retrieve

Move the cursor to the Retrieve menu item by using the RIGHT ARROW key and then press the ENTER key to select the Retrieve choice from the Assistant Main Menu. This will bring up the Retrieve menu of choices that will allow display and manipulation of the database. The Retrieve menu is displayed in figure 1.8.

Figure 1.8. The Retrieve Menu.

Display

Press the ENTER key to select the default menu choice of Display because you wish to take a look at the database records that you have created. The Display command has several options. You can display the entire database with all of the fields, display just some of the fields, or display just some of the records. After you have used the various display options, press the UP ARROW to move back to the Assistant Main Menu that is displayed in figure 1.9.

Figure 1.9. Assistant Main Menu.

HELP

You may press function key F1 at any time and receive context sensitive help from the dBASE III program. If you press the *F1 function* key in the Assist program, you will be presented with a navagational guide that shows where you are in the Assist menu maze. Your current position is marked by an arrow head to the left of the menu item you are currently using.

LEAVING ASSIST

Press the UP ARROW key to move up to the Assistant Main Menu. Press the UP ARROW key again and move up to the Assistant menu instructions screen. You will press the ESC key to leave Assist.

LEAVING dBASE III

To leave dBASE III, enter the *Quit command* and press ENTER. You will be returned to the DOS program.

THE IBM PC KEYBOARD

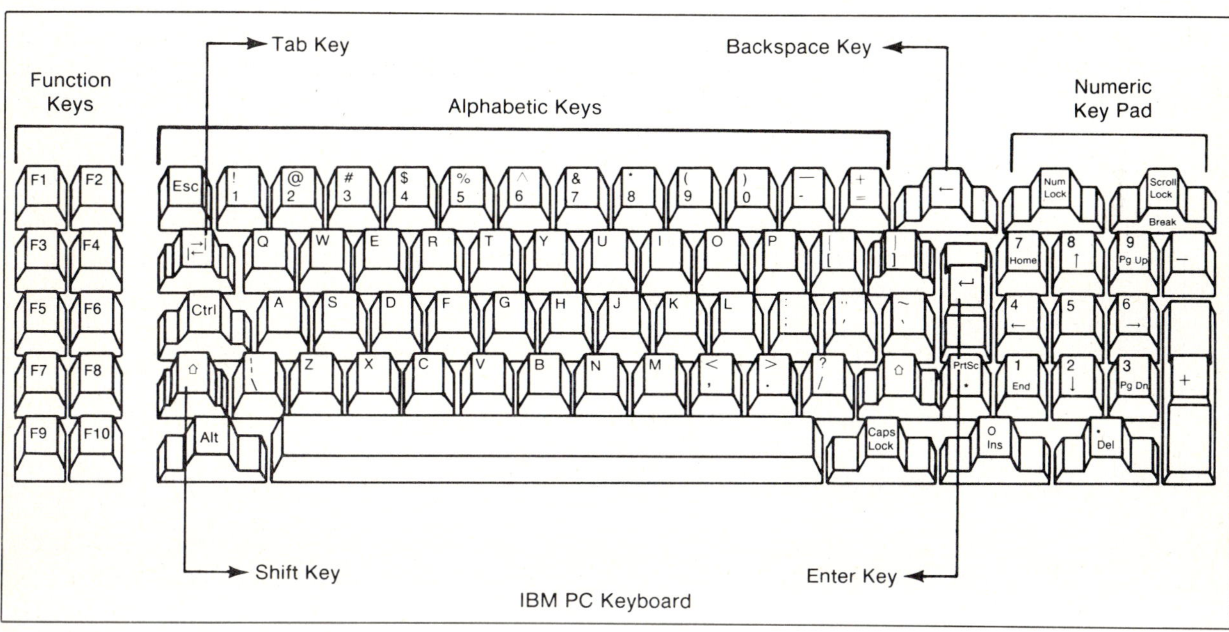

Figure 1.10. The IBM PC Keyboard.

Alphabetic keyboard	Contains the normal typewriter keys–the alphabetic keys (A-Z), the number keys (0-9), and some special character keys. These keys are all cream colored.
Function keys	These keys are assigned special commands by the dBASE III program. Each function key replaces a dBASE III command. These keys are all dark gray in color.
Numeric keypad keys	These keys are used for cursor movement by the dBASE III program. These keys are all cream colored.
Control keys	These keys are not found on a typewriter keyboard and are identified separately on the next page. These keys are all dark gray in color.

Left-hand side control keys

ESC key	This key is used to Escape from a dBASE III command.
CTRL key	This key is used like a shift key. You must press this key down, keep it pressed down, and then tap an alphabetic key. The symbol ^ is used to represent the CTRL key.
Left SHIFT key	The left SHIFT key is represented by a single upward pointing arrow. There are two SHIFT keys, one on the left-hand side of the alphabetic keyboard and one on the right-hand side of the alphabetic keyboard. The SHIFT key is used to capitalize an alphabetic character. The SHIFT key must also be used when you want to enter the upper character on a two character key. For example, to enter the ! character, you must press the SHIFT key and the 1 key at the same time.

Right-hand side control keys

Backspace key	Represented by a single left-pointing arrow, this key may be used to back up one character at a time in a command.
ENTER key	Represented by a single left-pointing arrow with a short vertical upstroke on the end of the arrow, this key is often used to send information to dBASE III. You will type in some information needed to complete a command and then press the ENTER key.
Right SHIFT key	Represented by a single up-pointing arrow, this key is used exactly like the left SHIFT key.
CAPS LOCK key	This key is used when you want to capitalize several letters in a row.

TUTORIAL EXPLANATION

You are now going to do the first of four tutorial lessons. These lessons will be done using the IBM PC (or compatible) computer. To follow the tutorial steps accurately you should be aware of the following:

1. Each step that you must follow is numbered in order. You must enter each step in the sequence indicated.

2. The information that you must enter is printed in **boldface.** You will key in exactly what is shown in **boldface.** An example would be—You press: **h.** This step indicates that you must press the *h* key. All the information that you must enter is shown in lowercase. You may actually use lowercase or uppercase.

3. The dBASE III program often responds with what is known as a *prompt.* This is a request for information. You must supply an answer to dBASE III. dBASE III prompts are always shown in UPPERCASE. An example of a prompt is the following: ENTER NAME OF FILE TO COPY TO.

4. In many cases you must complete the entry of information by pressing the ENTER key. The tutorial will always indicate that the ENTER key must be pressed by this statement: **{Press ENTER key}.** When you are not told to press the ENTER key, do not press it.

5. Whenever you are required to press one of the Control keys (ESC, TAB, CTRL, or ENTER), these keys will always be represented in ALL CAPS.

6. After you have completed a step in the tutorial, be sure to read the material enclosed in brackets "[ ]." This material tells you what you have done and sometimes provides checkpoints to make sure that you have completed the step successfully. Explanation of what you have done usually appears below each step.

7. There is a keyboard diagram (figure 1.10) and keyboard explanation in this chapter. Refer to this diagram if you cannot locate a key.

8. The symbol "^" will often be used to represent the CTRL key in the tutorial material.

9. After you have done some steps, the tutorial will often ask you to match your screen with a screen pictured in the tutorial. If your screen does not match the screen pictured in the tutorial, check with your instructor.

10. If you have a new diskette that you are going to use as your data diskette, (the diskette you will store your databases on), you must format this disk. Follow these steps to format the disk.
    a. Place the data disk in drive B.
    b. Place the DOS system disk in drive A.
    c. Make sure you have the DOS A> prompt.
    d. Enter: **format B:**   **{press ENTER key}**
    e. DOS will display the following prompt:

    ```
    INSERT A NEW DISKETTE FOR DRIVE B:
    AND STRIKE ANY KEY WHEN READY
    ```

    f. **{Press ENTER key}**
    g. DOS will display the following message:

    ```
    FORMATTING...
    ```

    [It will take about 40 seconds for DOS to format the diskette.]

    h. When the formatting procedure is completed, DOS will display the following prompt:

    ```
    FORMATTING... FORMAT COMPLETE

        362496 BYTES TOTAL DISK SPACE
        362496 BYTES AVAILABLE ON DISK

    FORMAT ANOTHER (Y/N)?
    ```

    i. You press: **n**
11. You only need to format the disk once, before you begin the first tutorial section.

Starting DOS

In this section of the tutorial, you will load DOS into RAM.

1.   Put the disk marked "Preboot DISK" in drive A.

2.   Put the disk marked "DATA DISK" in drive B.

3.   If the computer is turned off, turn it on and go to step 6.
     [This will perform a "cold boot" and load DOS into RAM.]

4.   If the computer is turned on, you will hold down the CTRL key, the ALT key, and press the DEL key.
     [This key sequence performs a "warm boot," which reads the DOS program into RAM.]

5.   Release the keys.

6.   DOS responds with:

     ```
     CURRENT DATE IS TUE 1-01-1980

     ENTER NEW DATE:
     ```

7.   Press: **ENTER key**

8.   DOS responds with:

     ```
     CURRENT TIME IS 0:01:14:20

     ENTER NEW TIME:
     ```

9.   Press: **ENTER key**

10. DOS responds with:

     ```
     THE IBM PERSONAL COMPUTER DOS

     VERSION 2.10 (C) COPYRIGHT IBM CORP 1981, 1982, 1983

     A>
     ```

     [This is the DOS prompt, indicating that you are in DOS and are logged to drive A.]

Starting dBASE III

In this section of the tutorial, you will load dBASE III into RAM. The dBASE III program will then display the dot prompt.

1.   Place the dBASE III diskette in drive A. Put the Preboot diskette back in its sleeve.

2. You Enter: `dbase`   {press ENTER key}

[This command reads the dBASE III program into RAM. The dot prompt should be displayed at the bottom of the screen. Your screen should match figure 1.11.] It will be similar if you are using the educational (DEMO) version.

```
dBASE III  version 1.00  14 June 1984 IBM/MSDOS ***

COPYRIGHT (c) ASHTON-TATE 1984
AS AN UNPUBLISHED LICENSED PROPRIETARY WORK.
ALL RIGHTS RESERVED.

Use  of  this software and the other materials contained  in  the
software  package  (the  "Materials") has been provided  under  a
Software  License Agreement (please read in  full).  In  summary,
Ashton-Tate  grants you a  paid-up, non-transferrable,  personal
license  to use the Materials only on a single or subsequent (but
not  additional) computer terminal for fifty years from the  time
the sealed diskette has been opened. You receive the right to use
the Materials,  but you do not become the owner of them.  You may
not alter,  decompile,  or reverse-assemble the software, and YOU
MAY  NOT  COPY  the Materials.  The Materials  are  protected  by
copyright,  trade secrets,  and trademark law,  the violation  of
which can result in civil damages and criminal prosecution.

dBASE, dBASE III and ASHTON-TATE are trademarks of Ashton-Tate.

Press the F1 key for help
Type a command (or ASSIST) and press the return key (↵) (Y).
```

Figure 1.11. Initial dBASE III Screen.

Starting Assist

1. Enter: `assist`   {press ENTER key}

[Loads in the dBASE III assistant program. The dBASE III assistant screen should be displayed. Your screen should match figure 1.12.]

```
                          The dBASE III
                           Assistant

      Assist uses menus to bring you the power of dBASE III


     ------------------------------------------------------------
        KEY                          FUNCTION
     ------------------------------------------------------------
     Esc                      Exit from current operation
     Up arrow                 Move to previous menu
     Down arrow               Move to next menu
     Left arrow               Move one item to the left
     Right arrow              Move one item to the right
     Home                     Go to first menu
     End                      Go to right most item
     Option Letter            Executes option (Unless otherwise noted
                              option letter is first letter of option)
     ------------------------------------------------------------


     Press DOWN ARROW (or ENTER) TO CONTINUE, ESC to EXIT ASSIST:
```

Figure 1.12. Assistant Main Menu.

2.   Press: **ENTER key**

[You have just pressed the ENTER key to continue with the Assist program. The Assistant Main Menu is displayed and should match figure 1.13.]

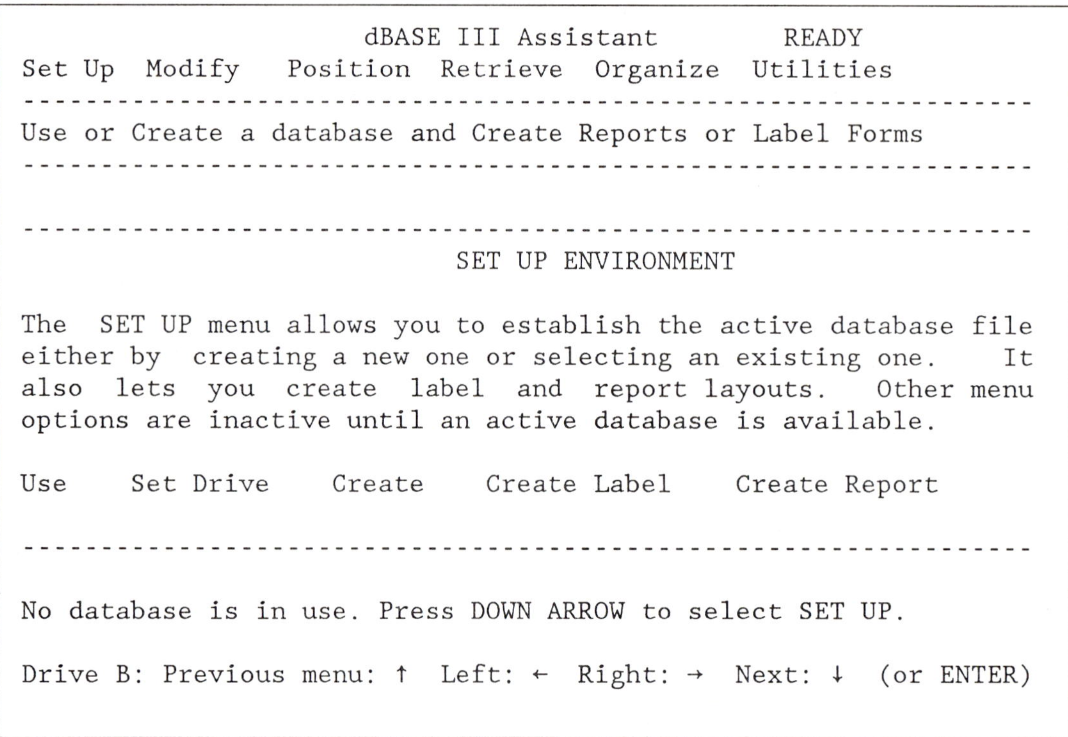

```
                    dBASE III Assistant          READY
     Set Up  Modify   Position Retrieve  Organize  Utilities
     ------------------------------------------------------------
     Use or Create a database and Create Reports or Label Forms
     ------------------------------------------------------------


     ------------------------------------------------------------
                         SET UP ENVIRONMENT

     The  SET UP menu allows you to establish the active database file
     either by  creating a new one or selecting an existing one.    It
     also  lets  you  create  label  and  report layouts.   Other menu
     options are inactive until an active database is available.


     Use     Set Drive    Create     Create Label     Create Report


     ------------------------------------------------------------


     No database is in use. Press DOWN ARROW to select SET UP.

     Drive B: Previous menu: ↑  Left: ←  Right: →  Next: ↓  (or ENTER)
```

Figure 1.13. Assistant Main Menu.

Create a Database

The message at the bottom of the screen tells you that no database is in use. You now have to create a database. Creating a database involves giving a name to your database and then entering the fields that you want the database to include. After you have entered all of the fields for your database you have created the database structure.

1. Press: **ENTER key**

    [You have pressed the ENTER key to select the default Assistant Main Menu item of Set Up. Your screen should display the Set Up menu as illustrated in figure 1.14.]

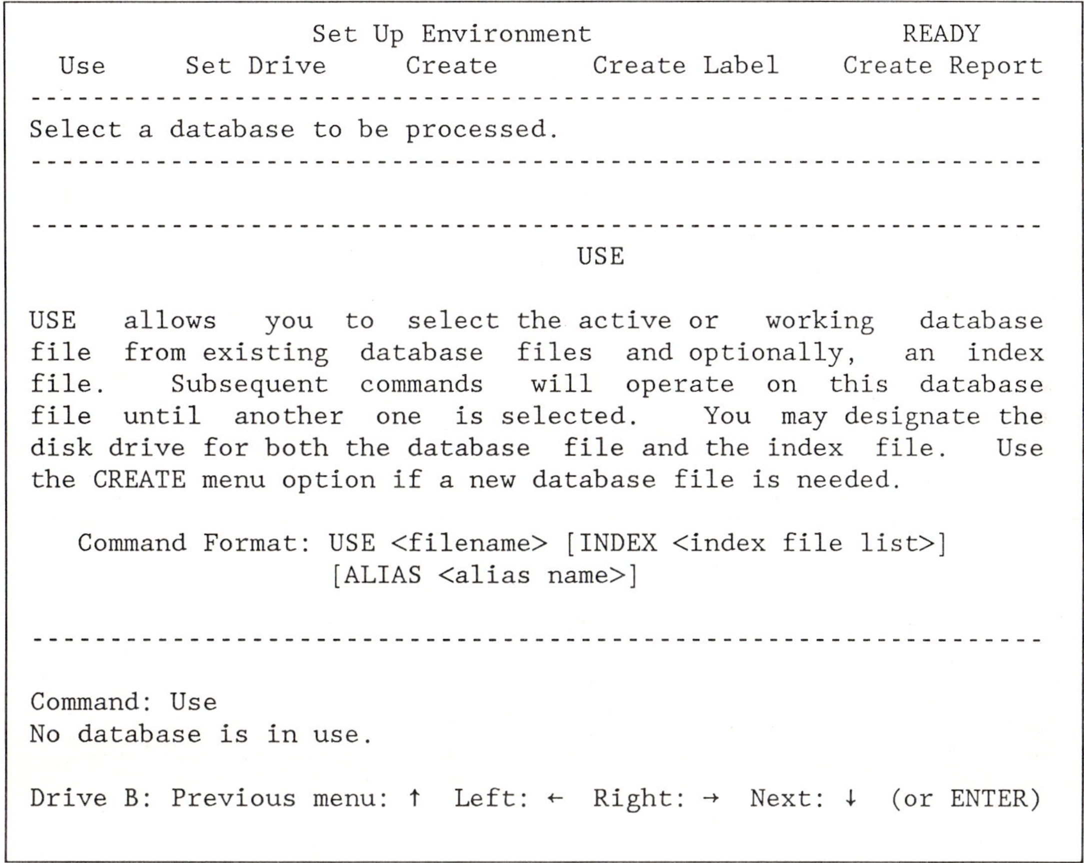

Figure 1.14. Set Up Menu.

2. Press: **RIGHT ARROW key twice**

    [You have pressed the RIGHT ARROW key twice to highlight the menu item Create a database. Read the message on Create that is displayed in figure 1.15.]

```
          Set Up Environment                          READY
 Use      Set Drive      Create        Create Label      Create Report
 -----------------------------------------------------------------------
 Create a database  (C--Option letter)
 -----------------------------------------------------------------------


 -----------------------------------------------------------------------
                              CREATE

 CREATE   is  used to produce a new database file.    It lets  you
 define  the structure of database records and  optionally,  start
 entering information.

              Command Format:   CREATE <filename>

 -----------------------------------------------------------------------


 Command: Create
 No database is in use.

 Drive B: Previous menu: ↑  Left: ←  Right: →  Next: ↓  (or ENTER)
```

Figure 1.15. Create Menu.

3.   Press: **ENTER key**

[You have just pressed the ENTER key to select the menu item Create. The filename screen should be displayed on your screen and should match figure 1.16.]

```
          Set Up Environment
 Use      Set Drive    Create      Create Label      Create Report
 -----------------------------------------------------------------------
 Create a database  (C--Option letter)
 -----------------------------------------------------------------------


 -----------------------------------------------------------------------
 A filename can consist of from 1 to 8 letters or digits.  A disk
 drive  letter  (A,B..)  and a colon can precede  the  filename.
 Otherwise,  current disk drive is used.     Enter the name of the
 file: [          ]
 -----------------------------------------------------------------------
 Command: Create
 No database is in use.

 Drive B: Previous menu: ↑  Left: ←  Right: →  Next: ↓  (or ENTER)
```

Figure 1.16. Display of Filename Screen.

4.   Enter: **widget**   {press ENTER key}

[You have just given a name to the new database file you are about to create. The field menu appears on the screen and should match figure 1.17.]

```
 B:widget.dbf                              Bytes remaining:    4000
                                           Fields defined:        0


 --------------------------------------------------------------------
 : CURSOR   ←    →   :      INSERT    :     DELETE    :Up a field:    ↑ :
 :  Char:   ←  →     :   Char: Ins  :  Char:  Del  :Down a field: ↓ :
 :  Word: Home End   :   Field: ^N  :  Word:   ^Y   :Exit/Save:  ^End:
 :  Pan:   ^←  ^→    :              :  Field: ^U   :Abort:        Esc:
 --------------------------------------------------------------------


 field name   type      width   dec
 -----------------------------------------
    1  [      ]   Char/text  [      ]  [      ]


Names start with a letter;   the remainder may be letters, digits,
or underscore
```

Figure 1.17. Naming a Database File.

Create Fields

You are now going to create a database structure by entering the fields that you wish to be included in your database. You must tell dBASE III the name of your field, the type of field, and the width (number of characters long) of the field. The name of the field must begin with a letter, cannot exceed ten characters in width and the only special character that can be used in the name is the underscore, ( ).

You are going to create two character fields. Character fields can contain any character in the character set. You are also going to create one numeric field. Numeric fields can only contain numeric characters. You must also tell dBASE III how many decimal places you want in your numeric fields.

1.   Enter: **cust_num**   {press ENTER KEY}

[You have given a name to the Customer Number field.]

2.   Press: **c**

[You have told dBASE III that the cust_num field is a character field.]

3.   Enter: **3**   {press ENTER KEY}

[You have told dBASE III that the width of the cust_num field is 3 characters.]

4. Enter: **cust_name**   {press ENTER KEY}

[You have given a name to the Customer Name field.]

5. Press: **c**

[You have told dBASE III that the Customer Name field is a character field.]

6. Enter: **25**   {press ENTER KEY}

[You have told dBASE III that the width of the Customer Name field is 25 characters.]

7. Enter: **amount**   {press ENTER KEY}

[You have given a name to the Amount field.]

8. Press: **n**

[You have told dBASE III that the Amount field is a numeric field.]

9. Enter: **11**   {press ENTER KEY}

[You have told dBASE III that the length of the Amount field is 11 characters.]

10. Enter: **2**   {press ENTER KEY}

[You have told dBASE III that the Amount field contains 2 decimal places.]

11. Press: **^END**

[You have ended the field definition.]

12. dBASE will display the following prompt:

HIT RETURN TO CONFIRM--ANY OTHER KEY TO RESUME

13. Press: **ENTER key**

[The database structure is written to disk.]

Input Data to Database

dBASE III will now give you an opportunity to enter data into your database. You have given the name WIDGET to your database and have created three fields as the structure of your database, but you have no data in the database. You can enter data into the database now, or you can enter data at some other time.

1. dBASE will display the following prompt:

INPUT DATA RECORDS NOW? (Y/N)

2.   Press: **y**

[The Data Entry menu and data entry screen are displayed as illustrated in figure 1.18.]

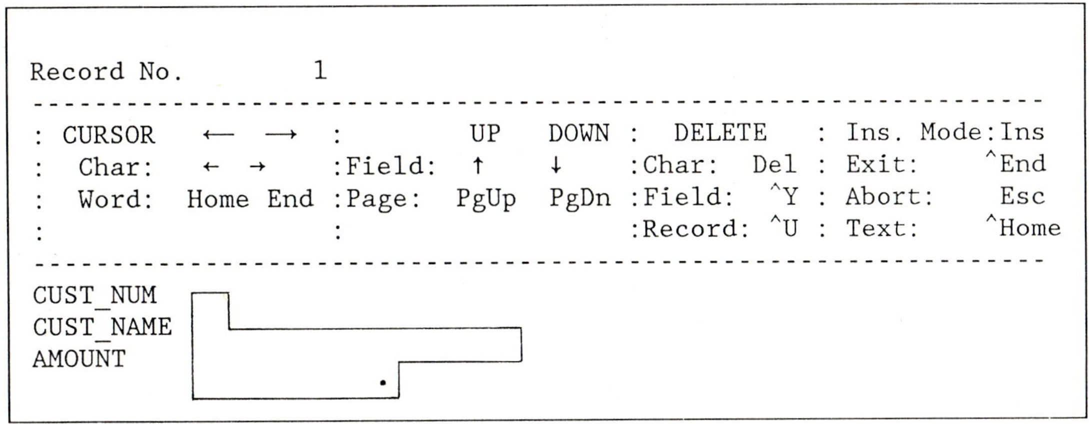

Figure 1.18. Data Entry Menu and Screen.

3.   Enter: **1**   {press ENTER KEY}

4.   Enter: **Deloren Corporation**   {press ENTER KEY}

5.   Enter: **9000**   {press ENTER KEY}

[You have completed the entry of record #1. dBASE III will now display a blank data entry screen for record #2.]

6.   Enter: **2**   {press ENTER KEY}

7.   Enter: **Al Capone Enterprises**   {press ENTER KEY}

8.   Enter: **65000**   {press ENTER KEY}

[You have completed the entry of record #2. dBASE III will now display a blank data entry screen for record #3.]

9.   Enter: **3**   {press ENTER KEY}

10.   Enter: **Sidereal Systems**   {press ENTER KEY}

11.   Enter: **28000**   {press ENTER KEY}

[You have completed the entry of record #3. dBASE III will now display a blank data entry screen for record #4.]

12.   Press: **^END**

[You have pressed ^END to end the data entry step. The Set Up menu should be displayed as illustrated in figure 1.19. Notice that the file in use is now b:widget.]

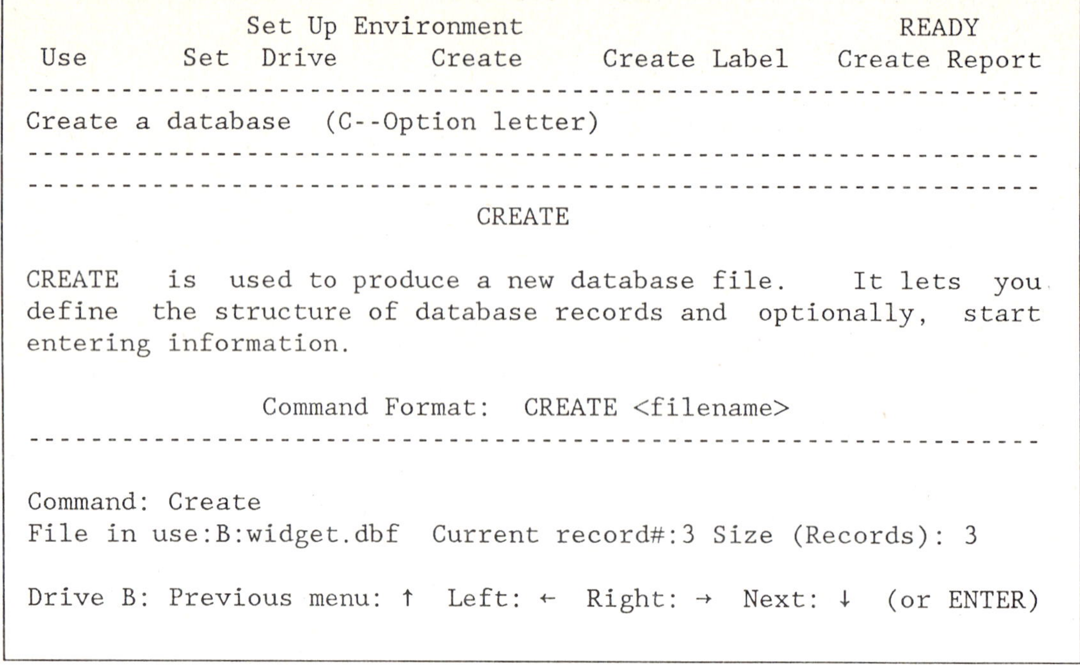

```
                Set Up Environment                          READY
    Use        Set Drive        Create      Create Label   Create Report
--------------------------------------------------------------------------
Create a database  (C--Option letter)
--------------------------------------------------------------------------
--------------------------------------------------------------------------
                               CREATE

CREATE    is  used to produce a new database file.    It lets  you
define   the structure of database records and  optionally,   start
entering information.

              Command Format:   CREATE <filename>
--------------------------------------------------------------------------

Command: Create
File in use:B:widget.dbf  Current record#:3 Size (Records): 3

Drive B: Previous menu: ↑  Left: ←  Right: →  Next: ↓  (or ENTER)
```

Figure 1.19. The Set Up Menu for `widget.dbf`.

Change to Retrieve Menu

You are now going to use a new menu, the Retrieve menu, to display the records in your database. The Display command allows you to display all the records with all the fields, all the records with some of the fields, some of the records with all of the fields, and some of the records with some of the fields. You may also use the display command to display records that meet a specified criteria.

1.   Press: **UP ARROW key**

[The Assistant Main Menu should be displayed on your screen as illustrated in figure 1.20.]

2. Press: **RIGHT ARROW key three times**

[You have positioned the cursor on the Retrieve menu item. Read the Retrieve Message that is displayed on your screen. This message should match the message illustrated in figure 1.21.]

3.   Press: **ENTER key**

[You have pressed the ENTER key to select the Retrieve menu item. The Retrieve menu should be displayed as illustrated in figure 1.22. The cursor is positioned on the Display menu item. Read the message on Display.]

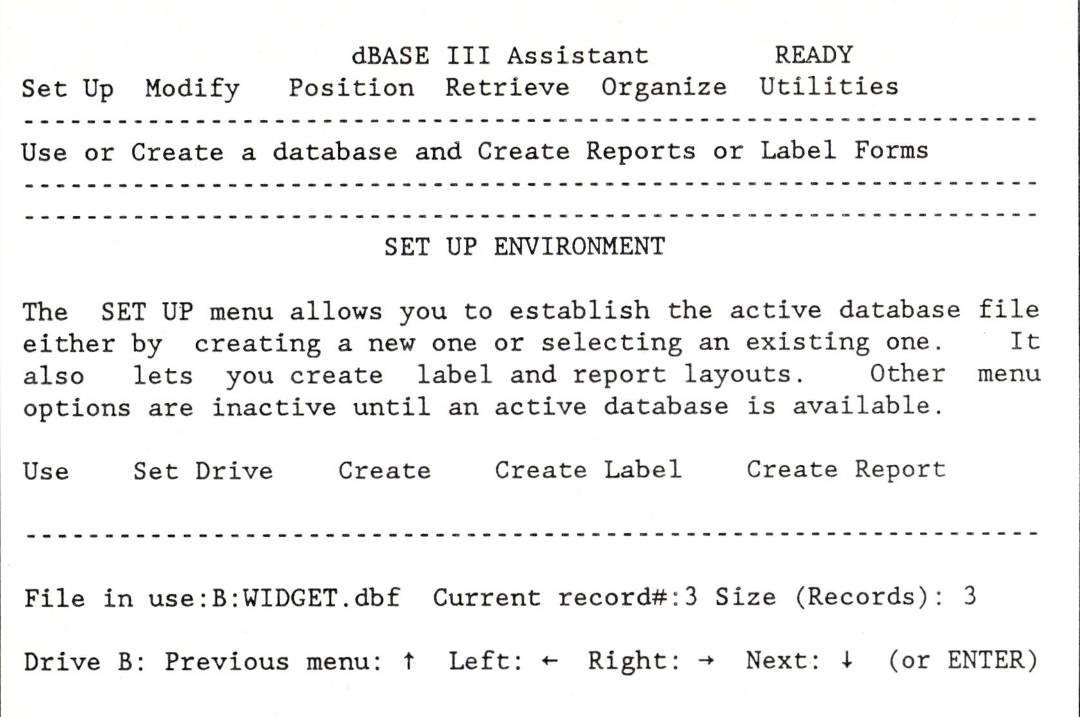
```
                    dBASE III Assistant            READY
Set Up  Modify   Position  Retrieve  Organize  Utilities
--------------------------------------------------------------
Use or Create a database and Create Reports or Label Forms
--------------------------------------------------------------

--------------------------------------------------------------
                    SET UP ENVIRONMENT

The  SET UP menu allows you to establish the active database file
either by  creating a new one or selecting an existing one.    It
also   lets  you create  label and report layouts.    Other  menu
options are inactive until an active database is available.

Use     Set Drive    Create     Create Label    Create Report

--------------------------------------------------------------

File in use:B:WIDGET.dbf  Current record#:3 Size (Records): 3

Drive B: Previous menu: ↑  Left: ←  Right: →  Next: ↓  (or ENTER)
```

Figure 1.20. Assistant Main Menu.

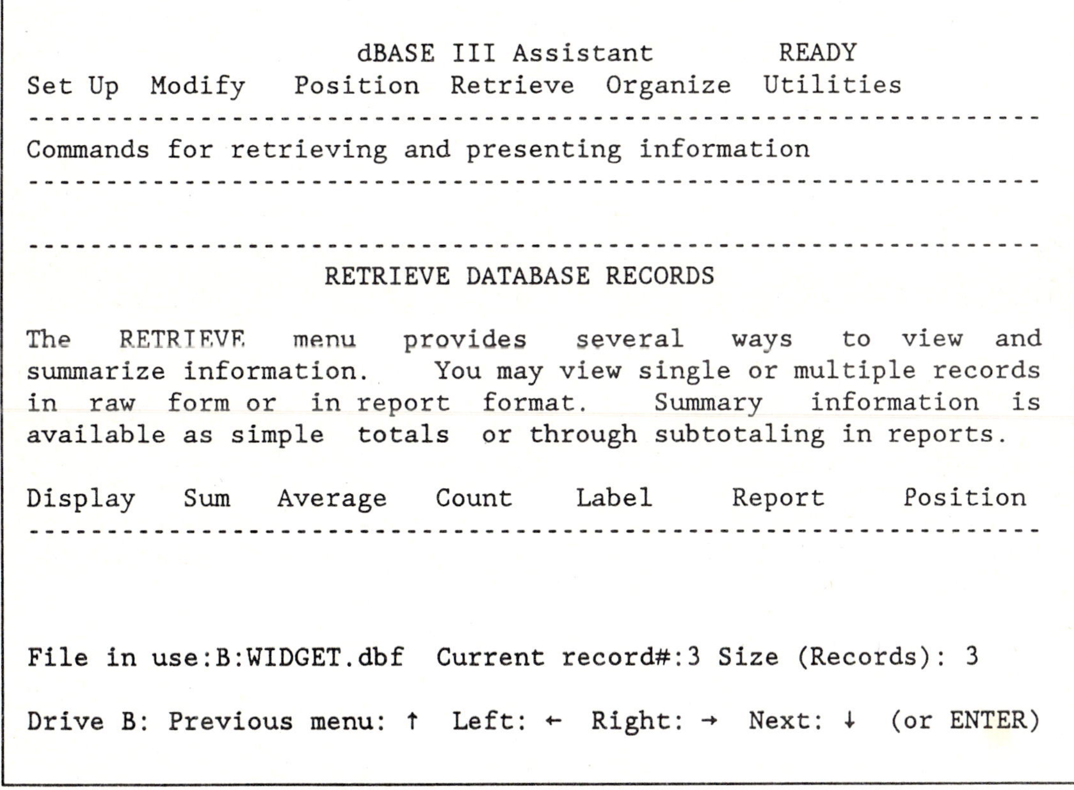
```
                    dBASE III Assistant            READY
Set Up  Modify   Position  Retrieve  Organize  Utilities
--------------------------------------------------------------
Commands for retrieving and presenting information
--------------------------------------------------------------

--------------------------------------------------------------
                  RETRIEVE DATABASE RECORDS

The   RETRIEVE  menu   provides   several   ways   to  view  and
summarize information.    You may view single or multiple records
in  raw  form  or  in report  format.    Summary  information  is
available  as simple  totals  or through subtotaling in reports.

Display   Sum   Average   Count    Label     Report     Position
--------------------------------------------------------------




File in use:B:WIDGET.dbf  Current record#:3 Size (Records): 3

Drive B: Previous menu: ↑  Left: ←  Right: →  Next: ↓  (or ENTER)
```

Figure 1.21. The Retrieve Menu.

```
        Retrieve and Present Information                        READY
Display  Sum  Average  Count  Label  Report    Position
- - - - - - - - - - - - - - - - - - - - - - - - - - - - - - - - - - - - - - - -
Display selected data in current database
- - - - - - - - - - - - - - - - - - - - - - - - - - - - - - - - - - - - - - - -

                               DISPLAY

DISPLAY  shows  requested information from  the  active  database
file.   You  can specify which records should be shown  and  what
information within the records to include.

    Command Format: DISPLAY [<scope>] [<expression list>]
              [FOR / WHILE <condition>] [OFF] [TO PRINT]


- - - - - - - - - - - - - - - - - - - - - - - - - - - - - - - - - - - - - - -


Command: Display
File in use:B:WIDGET.dbf Current record #: 3 Size (records):   3

Drive B: Previous menu: ↑  Left: ←  Right: →  Next: ↓  (or ENTER)
```

Figure 1.22. Display Menu Screen.

Display Record Commands

You are now going to use the Display commands. It is important that you follow the command line. Found at the bottom of the screen, the command line will begin with the following:

    Command:Display

The rest of the command will be built up step by step as you move through the menu items. Check the command line after you complete each step.

Display All Records

In this section of the tutorial, you are going to learn how to use the Display All command to display all of the records in a file on the screen.

1.   Press: **ENTER key**

      [You have pressed the ENTER key to select the Display menu item. The first Display screen should be displayed as illustrated in figure 1.23.]

```
      Retrieve and Present Information
Display  Sum  Average  Count  Label  Report   Position
---------------------------------------------------------------
Select scope element
---------------------------------------------------------------
        ---------------------------------------------------------
        :             Process current record (no scope specified) :
        : NEXT        For the NEXT N records                       :
        : ALL         Process ALL the database records             :
        : RECORD      Process one specified record                 :
        ---------------------------------------------------------



Command: Display
File in use:B:WIDGET.dbf Current record #: 3 Size (records):    3

Drive B: Press ⟶ to move to next selection item.
```

Figure 1.23. Display Menu Screen.

2. **Press: DOWN ARROW twice**

[You have moved the cursor to the "Process ALL the database records" choice.]

3. **Press: ENTER key**

[You have pressed the ENTER key to select the choice "Display ALL database records." Your screen should display the second display screen and should match figure 1.24. Notice that the command line now shows: Command:Display ALL.]

```
      Retrieve and Present Information
Display  Sum  Average  Count  Label  Report   Position
---------------------------------------------------------------
Select conditional statement if desired
---------------------------------------------------------------
        ---------------------------------------------------------
        :             ⟶ Continue to next item ⟶                  :
        : FOR         Every record that satisfies condition        :
        : WHILE       Until a record no longer satisfies condition :
        ---------------------------------------------------------


Command: Display  ALL
File in use:B:WIDGET.dbf Current record #: 3 Size (records):    3

Drive B: Press ⟶ to move to next selection item.
```

Figure 1.24. The "Display ALL Database Records" Screen

4. Press: **ENTER key**

[You have pressed the ENTER key to continue with the Display command. The third display screen
should be displayed and should match figure 1.25.]

<pre>
          Retrieve and Present Information
  Display Sum Average Count Label Report   Position
  -

  Select Field names—Position using ARROW KEYS—Select using ENTER:
  -

                    Field Name   Field Type   Width   Dec. #
                    CUST_NUM   Character   3
                    CUST_NAME   Character   25
                    AMOUNT   Numeric   11   2

  Command: Display ALL
  File in use:B:WIDGET.dbf Current record #: 3 Size (records):   3

  Drive B: Press ⟶ to move to next selection item.
</pre>

Figure 1.25. The Third Display Screen.

5. Press: **ENTER key three times**

[You have pressed the ENTER key three times to mark all three fields for display. An arrowhead
should appear to the left of each field name each time you press the ENTER key.]

6. Press: **RIGHT ARROW key once**

[All the records in your database should be displayed on your screen, and should match figure 1.26.
Notice that the command line has changed from "Display ALL" to "Display ALL FIELDS CUST_NUM,
CUST_NAME, AMOUNT."]

7. Press: **ENTER key**

[You have pressed the ENTER key to return to the Retrieve menu. Your screen should match figure
1.27.]

```
      Retrieve and Present Information
Display Sum Average Count Label Report  Position
-----------------------------------------------------------------

Select Field names-Position using ARROW KEYS-Select using ENTER:
-----------------------------------------------------------------


Record#  CUST_NUM  CUST_NAME                        AMOUNT
     1 1          Deloren Corporation             9000.00
     2 2          Al Capone Enterprises          65000.00
     3 3          Sidereal Systems               28000.00




Command: Display ALL   FIELDS CUST_NUM, CUST_NAME, AMOUNT
File in use:B:WIDGET.dbf Current record#:End of File Size:3

Drive B:     Press any Character To Continue
```

Figure 1.26. Displaying Records on a Data Screen.

```
      Retrieve and Present Information                    READY
Display Sum Average Count Label Report  Position
-----------------------------------------------------------------
Display selected data in current database
-----------------------------------------------------------------


                         DISPLAY

DISPLAY shows requested information from the  active database
file. You  can specify which records should be  shown  and  what
information within the records to include.

   Command Format: DISPLAY [<scope>] [<expression list>]
              [FOR / WHILE <condition>] [OFF] [TO PRINT]


-----------------------------------------------------------------

Command: Display
File in use:B:WIDGET.dbf Current record:End of file Size :3

Drive B: Previous menu: ↑  Left: ←  Right: →  Next: ↓  (or ENTER)
```

Figure 1.27. The Retrieve Menu.

In this section of the tutorial, you will learn how to use the Display All command to display all of the records on the screen, but only display some of the fields in each record. You can display any fields and can exclude any fields you wish from the display.

1.   Press: **ENTER key**

[You have pressed the ENTER key to select the Display menu item. The first Display screen should be displayed as illustrated in figure 1.28.]

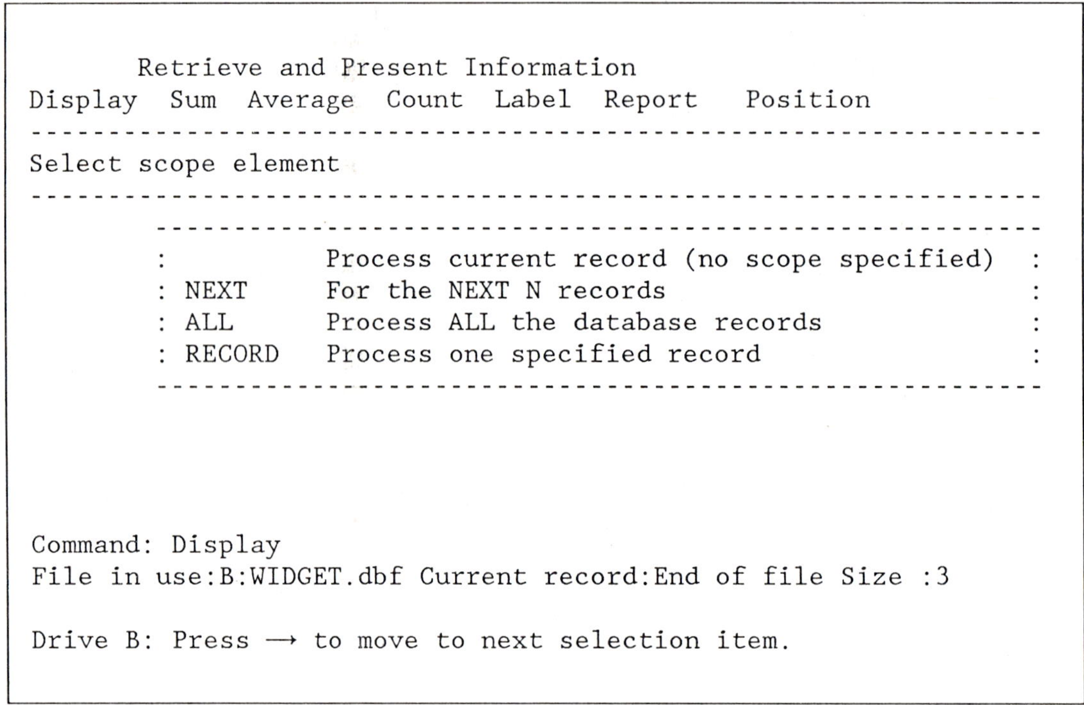

Figure 1.28. The Display Menu Screen.

2.   Press: **DOWN ARROW twice**

[You have moved the cursor to the "Process ALL the database records" choice.]

3.   Press: **ENTER key**

[You have pressed the ENTER key to select the choice "display ALL database records." Your screen should display the second display screen and should match figure 1.29. Notice that the command line now shows: Command:Display ALL.]

```
      Retrieve and Present Information
Display  Sum  Average  Count  Label  Report    Position
------------------------------------------------------------
Select conditional statement if desired
------------------------------------------------------------
      ------------------------------------------------------
      :              → Continue to next item →           :
      : FOR       Every record that satisfies condition  :
      : WHILE     Until a record no longer satisfies condition :
      ------------------------------------------------------




Command: Display  ALL
File in use:B:WIDGET.dbf Current record:End of file Size :3

Drive B: Press → to move to next selection item.
```

Figure 1.29. The Second Display Screen.

4. Press: **ENTER key**

[You have pressed the ENTER key to continue with the Display command. The third display screen should be displayed on your screen and should match figure 1.30.]

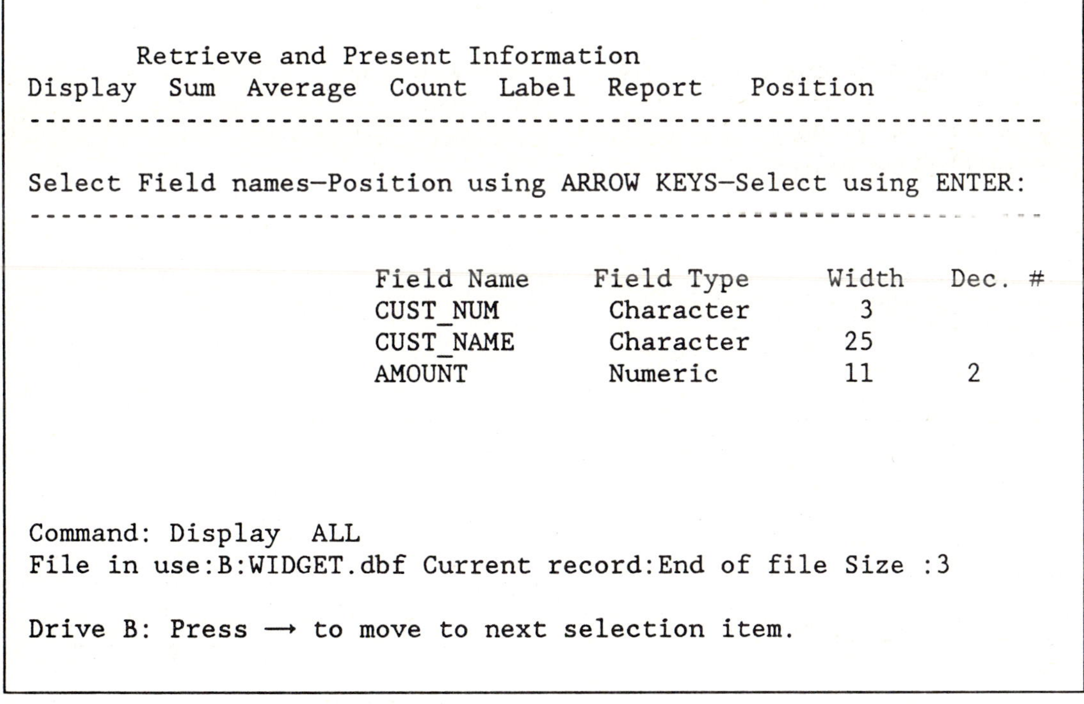

```
      Retrieve and Present Information
Display  Sum  Average  Count  Label  Report    Position
------------------------------------------------------------
Select Field names—Position using ARROW KEYS—Select using ENTER:
------------------------------------------------------------

              Field Name      Field Type     Width   Dec. #
              CUST_NUM        Character        3
              CUST_NAME       Character       25
              AMOUNT          Numeric         11       2




Command: Display  ALL
File in use:B:WIDGET.dbf Current record:End of file Size :3

Drive B: Press → to move to next selection item.
```

Figure 1.30. The Third Display Screen.

5.   Press: **DOWN ARROW key once**

[You have pressed the DOWN ARROW key once to skip the Customer Number field.]

6.   Press: **ENTER key**

[You have pressed the ENTER key to mark the Customer Name field for display. An arrowhead should appear to the left of the Customer Name field.]

7.   Press: **ENTER key**

[You have pressed the ENTER key to mark the Amount field for display. An arrowhead should appear to the left of the amount.]

8. Press: **RIGHT ARROW key once**

[You have pressed the RIGHT ARROW key to display the records in your database. Notice that only the Customer Name and the Amount fields are displayed at this time. Notice that the command line changed from "Display ALL" to "Display ALL FIELDS CUST_NAME, AMOUNT." Your screen should match figure 1.31.]

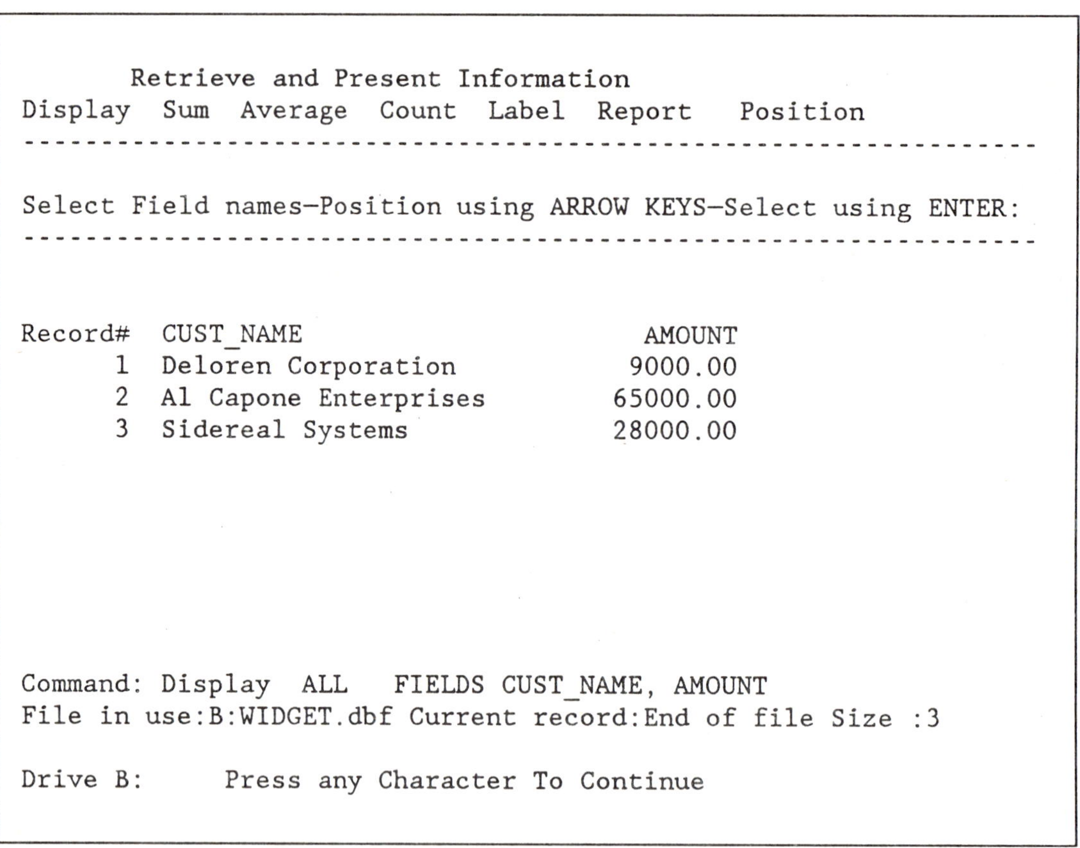

Figure 1.31.   The Third Display Screen.

9.   Press: **ENTER key**

[You have pressed the ENTER key to return to the Retrieve menu.]

In this section of the tutorial, you will learn how to select a single record for display upon the screen.

1. Press: **ENTER key**

    [You have pressed the ENTER key to select the display menu item. The first display screen should be displayed as illustrated in figure 1.32.]

```
         Retrieve and Present Information
   Display  Sum  Average  Count  Label  Report   Position
   ---------------------------------------------------------------
   Select scope element
   ---------------------------------------------------------------
         --------------------------------------------------------
         :              Process current record (no scope specified)  :
         : NEXT         For the NEXT N records                       :
         : ALL          Process ALL the database records             :
         : RECORD       Process one specified record                 :
         --------------------------------------------------------



   Command: Display
   File in use:B:WIDGET.dbf Current record:End of file Size :3

   Drive B: Press → to move to next selection item.
```

Figure 1.32. The Display Menu Screen.

2. Press: **DOWN ARROW key three times**

    [You have pressed the DOWN ARROW key three times to move the cursor to the "Process one specified record" choice.]

3. Press: **ENTER key**

    [You have pressed the ENTER key to select the Record menu item.]

4. dBASE III displays the following prompt:

    ENTER NUMERIC VALUE:

5. Enter: **1**   {press ENTER KEY}

    [You have entered a value of 1 to select record #1.]

6.   Press: **ENTER key**

[You have pressed the ENTER key to continue with the Display command. The third display screen should be displayed on your screen and should match figure 1.33.]

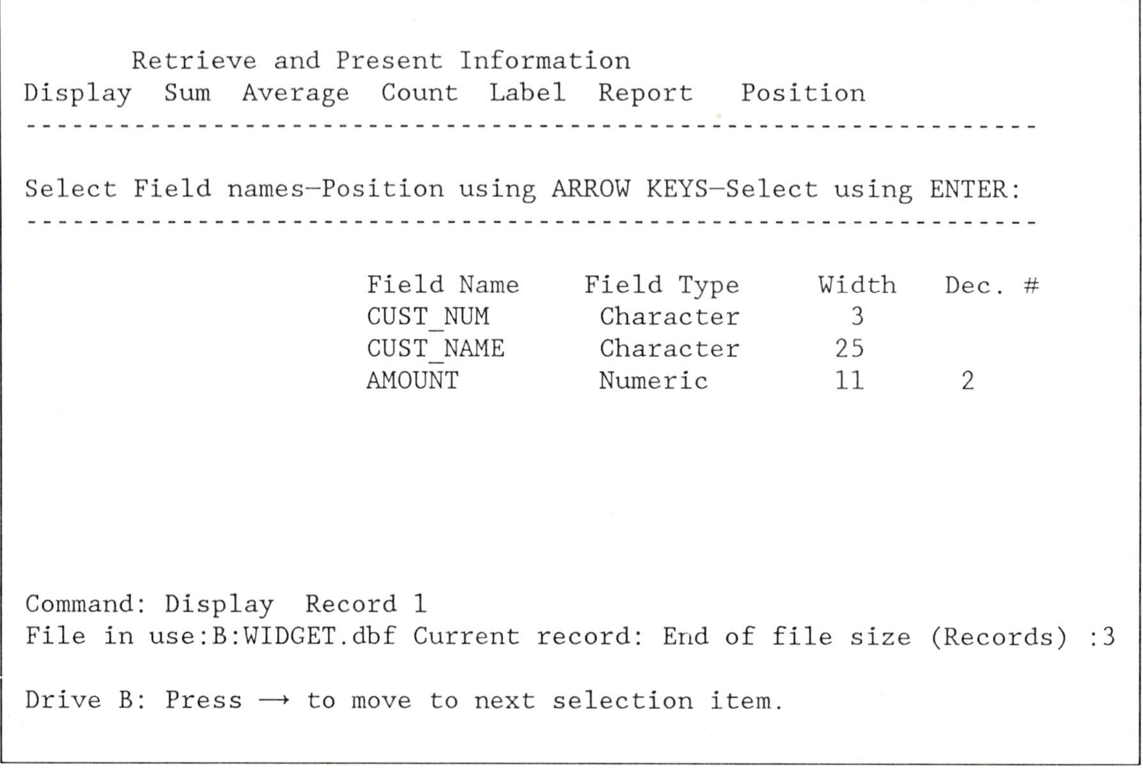

Figure 1.33. The Third Display Screen.

7.   Press: **ENTER key three times**

[You have pressed the ENTER key three times to mark all three fields for display. An arrowhead should appear to the left of each field name after you press the ENTER key.]

8.   Press: **RIGHT ARROW key once**

[Only record #1 should be displayed. Your screen should match figure 1.34. Notice that the command line displays Display RECORD 1 FIELDS CUST_NUM, CUST_NAME, AMOUNT.]

9.   Press: **ENTER key**

[You have pressed the ENTER key to return to the Retrieve menu.]

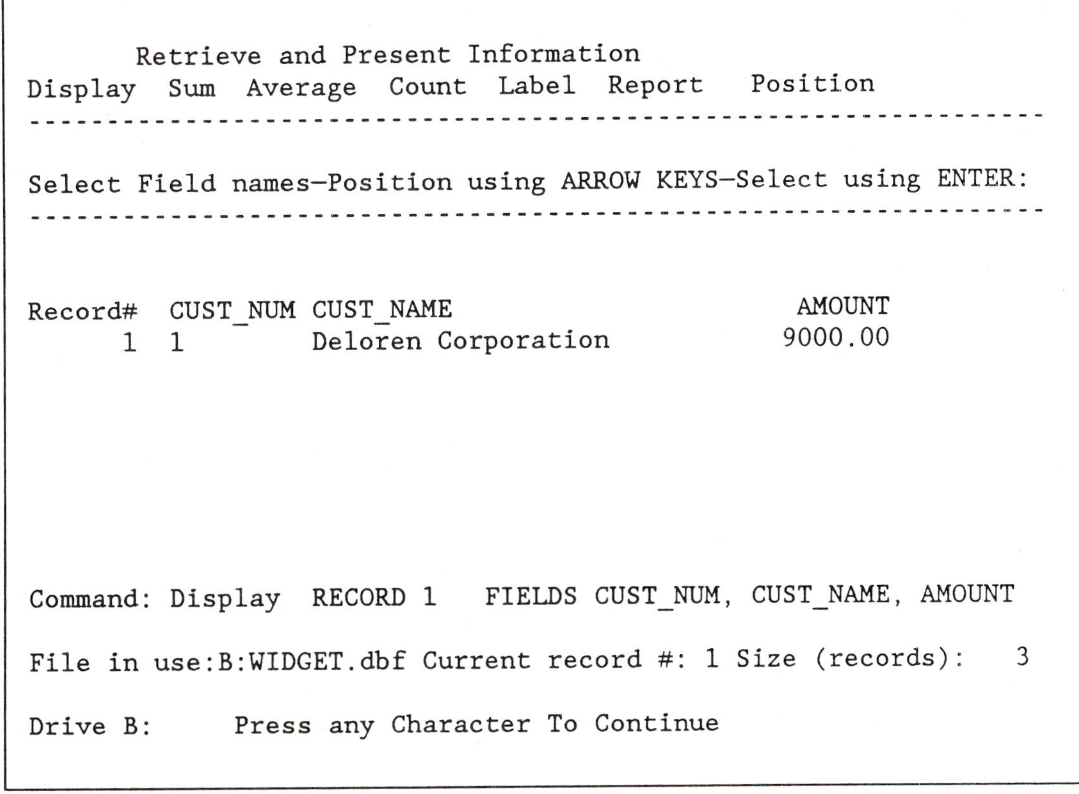

Figure 1.34. Displaying One Record.

Display Certain Records

In this section of the tutorial, you will learn how to enter a criteria so that you may selectively display records upon the screen.

1. Press: **ENTER key**

    [You have pressed the ENTER key to accept the default Retrieve menu item of Display.]

2. Press: **DOWN ARROW twice**

    [You have pressed the DOWN ARROW twice to move the cursor to the "ALL records processed" menu item.]

3. Press: **ENTER key**

    [You have pressed the ENTER key to select the "ALL records processed" menu item. Your screen should match figure 1.35.]

```
          Retrieve and Present Information
   Display  Sum  Average  Count  Label  Report    Position
   ---------------------------------------------------------------
   Select conditional statement if desired
   ---------------------------------------------------------------
           ------------------------------------------------------
           :                  → Continue to next item →         :
           : FOR       Every record that satisfies condition    :
           : WHILE     Until a record no longer satisfies condition :
           ------------------------------------------------------




   Command: Display  ALL
   File in use:B:WIDGET.dbf Current record #: 1 Size (records):   3

   Drive B: Press → to move to next selection item.
```

Figure 1.35. "ALL Records Processed" Menu Item.

4. Press: **DOWN ARROW key once**

[You have pressed the DOWN ARROW key once to move the cursor to the "FOR every record that satisfies a condition" menu choice.]

5. Press: **ENTER key**

[You have pressed the ENTER key to select the "FOR every record that satisfies a condition" menu item. Your screen should match figure 1.36. Notice that the command line shows DISPLAY ALL FOR.]

6. Press: **DOWN ARROW twice**

[Pressed the DOWN ARROW twice to move the cursor to the Amount field.]

7. Press: **ENTER key**

[You have pressed the ENTER key to select the Amount field as your FOR field. Your screen should match figure 1.37. Notice that the command line shows Display ALL FOR AMOUNT.]

```
       Retrieve and Present Information
Display  Sum  Average  Count  Label  Report   Position
- - - - - - - - - - - - - - - - - - - - - - - - - - - - - - - - - - - - - - - -

Select Field names—Position using ARROW KEYS—Select using ENTER:
- - - - - - - - - - - - - - - - - - - - - - - - - - - - - - - - - - - - - - - -

                        Field Name     Field Type     Width    Dec. #
                        CUST_NUM       Character        3
                        CUST_NAME      Character        25
                        AMOUNT         Numeric          11        2




Command: Display  ALL FOR
File in use:B:WIDGET.dbf Current record #: 1 Size (records):    3
```

Figure 1.36. "FOR Every Record that Satisfies a Condition" Menu Item.

```
        Retrieve and Present Information
Display  Sum  Average  Count  Label  Report   Position
- - - - - - - - - - - - - - - - - - - - - - - - - - - - - - - - - - - - - - - -

Select Field names—Position using ARROW KEYS—Select using ENTER:
- - - - - - - - - - - - - - - - - - - - - - - - - - - - - - - - - - - - - - - -

   - - - - - - - - - - - - - - - - - - - - - - - -
   :  =         Equal to                         :
   :  <         Less than                         :
   :  >         Greater than                      :
   :  >=        Greater than or equal to :
   :  <=        Less than or equal to    :
   :  <>        Not equal to                      :
   - - - - - - - - - - - - - - - - - - - - - - - -


Command: Display  ALL FOR AMOUNT
File in use:B:WIDGET.dbf Current record #: 1 Size (records):    3
```

Figure 1.37. Selecting a FOR Field.

8. Press: **DOWN ARROW twice**

[You have pressed the DOWN ARROW key twice to move the cursor to the greater than (>) sign.]

9. Press: **ENTER key**

[You have pressed the ENTER key to select "amount greater than" as your condition. Notice that the command line now shows Display ALL FOR AMOUNT >]

10. dBASE III now displays the following prompt:

ENTER VALUE TO COMPARE:

11. Enter: **10000**   {**press ENTER KEY**}

[You have entered 10000 as the "amount greater than" figure. Notice that the command line shows Display ALL FOR AMOUNT > 1000.]

12. Press: **ENTER key**

[You have pressed the ENTER key to continue to the next screen. Your screen should match figure 1.38.]

```
         Retrieve and Present Information
   Display  Sum  Average  Count  Label  Report   Position
   ------------------------------------------------------------

   Select Field names—Position using ARROW KEYS—Select using ENTER:
   ------------------------------------------------------------

                   Field Name    Field Type    Width   Dec. #
                   CUST_NUM      Character       3
                   CUST_NAME     Character      25
                   AMOUNT        Numeric        11       2




   Command: Display  ALL FOR AMOUNT > 10000
   File in use:B:WIDGET.dbf Current record #:1 Size (Records):  3

   Drive B: Press  →  to move to next selection item.
```

Figure 1.38. Entering the Value.

13. Press: **DOWN ARROW key**

[You have pressed the DOWN ARROW key to skip the Customer Number field.]

14. Press: **ENTER key twice**

[You have pressed the ENTER key twice to mark the last two fields for display. An arrowhead should appear to the left of each field as you press ENTER.]

15. Press: **RIGHT ARROW key once**

[You have pressed the RIGHT ARROW key once to display the records that have an amount greater than 10000. Your screen should match figure 1.39. Only the two records that have an amount greater than 10000 are displayed.]

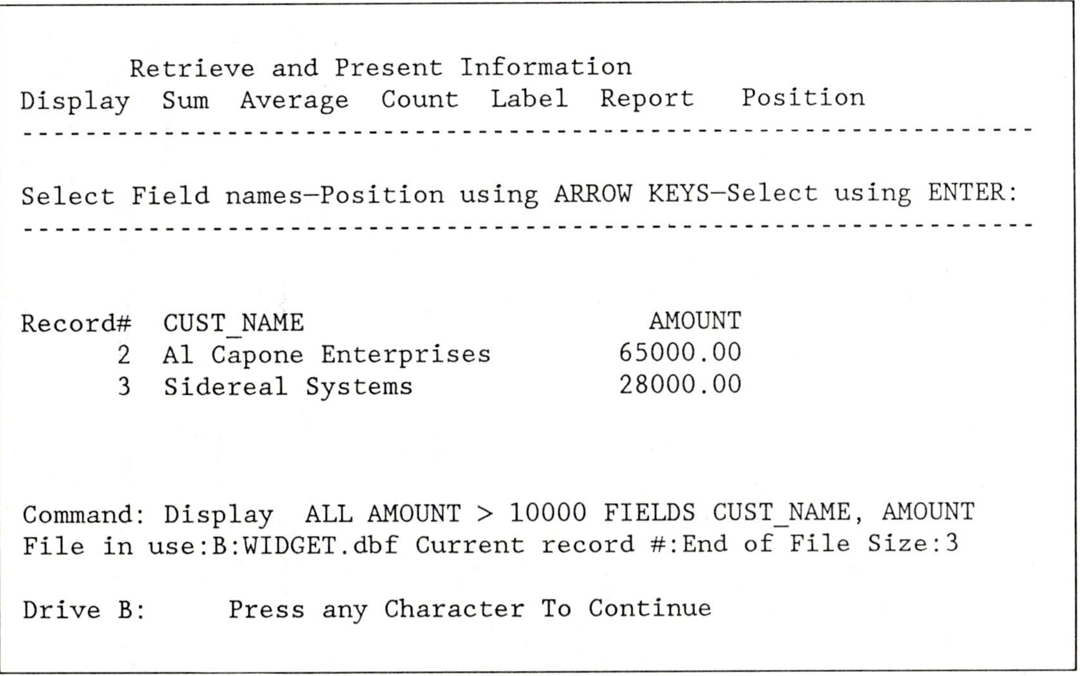

Figure 1.39. Display of Amounts Greater than 10000.

16. Press: **ENTER key**

[You have pressed the ENTER key to return to the Retrieve menu.]

Using the ESC Key to Escape

1. Press: **ENTER key**

[You have pressed the ENTER key to select the Display menu item. The first Display screen should be displayed on your screen.]

2. Press: **ESC key**

[You have pressed the ESC key to ESCape from the Display command. You are returned to the Retrieve menu.]

Navigational Guide

In this section of the tutorial, you will use the F1 function key to display a navagational guide that shows you where you are in the Assist menu maze. You can press the F1 key at any time.

1. Press: **F1 function key**

   [Your screen should match figure 1.40. Notice the arrowhead next to the Display command. The arrowhead always indicates your current position in the Assist menus. You can examine this menu at any time to determine where you need to move next.]

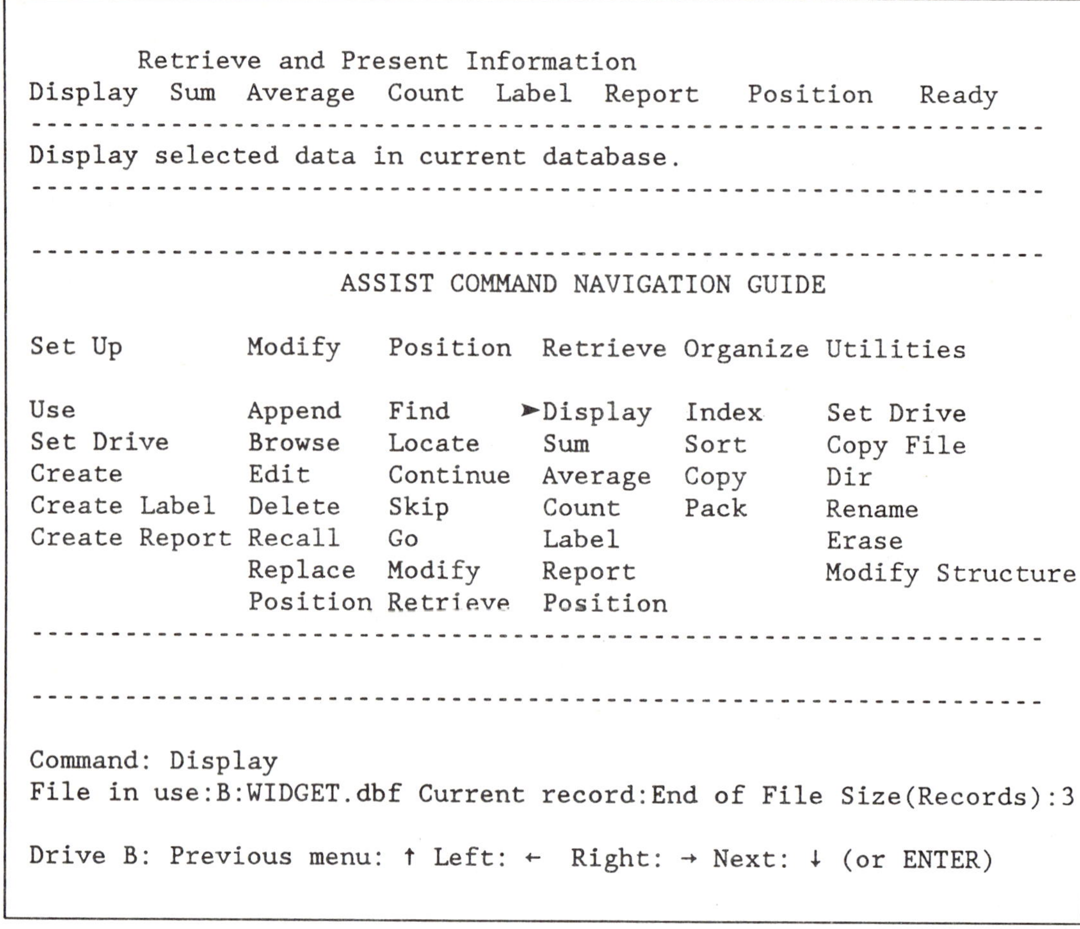

Figure 1.40. The Navigational Guide.

2. Press: **F1 function key**

   [You have pressed the F1 function key to leave the on-line help and return to the Assist program.]

Leaving Assist

In this section of the tutorial, you will learn how to leave the Assist program and return to the dBASE III program. All you have to do is press UP ARROW keys until you reach the Assist instruction screen.

1. Press: **UP ARROW key**

[You have pressed the UP ARROW key to move to the Assistant Main Menu.]

2. Press: **UP ARROW key**

[You have pressed the UP ARROW key to move up to the Assist Instruction screen.]

3. Press: **ESC key**

[You have pressed the ESC key to leave Assist and return to the dBASE III program. A dot prompt should be displayed on your screen.]

Leaving dBASE III

1. Enter: **quit**   {press ENTER KEY}

[You have entered the Quit command to leave dBASE III. The A> prompt should be displayed on your screen indicating that you have returned to DOS. You screen should match figure 1.41.]

```
  .quit
*** END RUN dBASE III
A>
```

Figure 1.41. Leaving Assist.

Commands Summary

Assist	Calls dBASE III assistant.
Create	This command is used to produce a new database file. It allows definition of the structure of database records and, optionally, entering information.
dBASE	Starts dBASE III program.
Display	This command shows requested information from the active database file. You can specify which records should be shown and what information within the records to include.
Quit	Command to leave dBASE III.
^END	Command to exit a dBASE III function.

Review of Menus

Assist Main Menu	Set Up Modify Position Retrieve Organize Utilities The Assist main menu is the gateway menu to all other menus in the Assist system.

Set Up Environment Menu

`Use   Set Drive   Create   Create Label   Create Report`
The SET UP menu allows you to establish the active database file either by creating a new one or by selecting an existing one. It also lets you create label and report layouts. Other menu options are inactive until an active database is available.

Retrieve Database Records Menu

`Display   Sum   Average   Count   Label   Report   Position`
The Retrieve menu provides several ways to view and summarize information. You may view single or multiple records in raw form or in report format. Summary information is available as simple totals or through sub totals in reports.

_____ 1. This command starts the dBASE III program.
    a. dbase III   b. dBase   c. dBase3

_____ 2. This command calls the dBASE III assistant.
    a. Assistant   b. Help   c. Assist

_____ 3. This command will exit dbase III and return you to DOS.
    a. End   b. Quit   c. ^END

_____ 4. This function key is used to ask for help.
    a. F1   b. F4   c. F6

_____ 5. This command is used to define a new database file.
    a. Create   b. Define   c. Start

_____ 6. This command will show requested information from the active database file.
    a. Display   b. Show   c. Help

_____ 7. This command is used to display every database record.
    a. Display For   b. Display All   c. Display Record

_____ 8. This command is used to selectively display database records based upon some criteria.
    a. Display ALL For   b. Display All   c. Display record

_____ 9. The command is built up item by item in the _____?
    a. Menu cursor   b. Help screen   c. Command line

_____ 10. This command generally allows you to leave a dBASE III function.
    a. ^END   b. Leave   c. Quit

1. Discuss the difference between a command driven program and a menu driven program.

2. Define a field, a record and a file.

3. Identify and discuss the two types of fields used in chapter 1.

4. Discuss the alternative techniques that can be used to select an Assist Menu item.

5. Discuss the basic technique involved in moving from one menu to another menu.

6. You can leave a dBASE III function (such as Adding Records to the file) by either pressing ^END or ESC. What is the difference between these methods?

2

dBASE III: Assist, Part 2

LEARNING OBJECTIVES

After completing chapter two the student will be able to:

1.   Utilize the Use command to select the active database.
2.   Become familiar with the commands on the Modify Database menu.
3.   Utilize the Append command to add records to the database.
4.   Utilize the Edit command to change information in one data record at a time.
5.   Utilize the Browse command to display a screen full of records.
6.   Utilize the Delete command to mark records for deletion.
7.   Utilize the Recall command to unmark records that were marked for deletion.
8.   Utilize the Pack command to remove records from the database file.
9.   Become familiar with the commands on the Organize Database menu.
10. Utilize the Sort command to reorder a database file.
11. Utilize the Copy command to copy a database file to another database file.

USE

A database called WIDGET was created by you using the tutorial in chapter 1. When you start dBASE III in the tutorial for this chapter, dBASE III will beep to tell you that no database has been selected. You will utilize a new command called the *Use command* to select the database WIDGET. If you have other databases that you have created, you may employ the Use command to select any of the databases as the *active database*. Once you have selected a database, you may then use the other dBASE III commands to manipulate this database.

Modify Database Menu

You will learn to use a new Assist menu called the *Modify Database menu*. The commands available on the Modify Database menu are illustrated in figure 2.1.

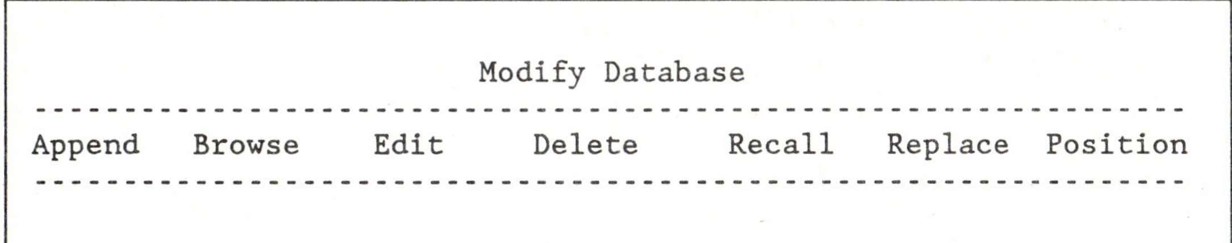

Figure 2.1. The Modify Database Menu.

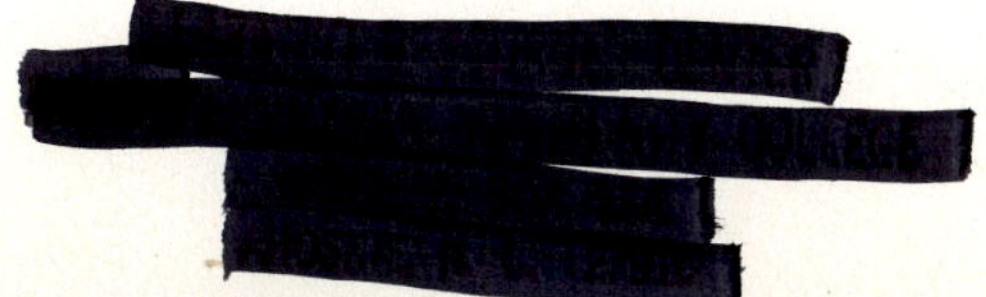

39

Append

The *Append command* allows you to add records to your database. You can add as many records as you like in each Append session, and you can use the Append command as often as you wish. In the tutorial, you will use the Append command to add one record.

Edit

The *Edit command* allows you to change the information in one specified record. You will select the Edit command and then indicate to dBASE III in which record you wish to make changes. You may edit records as often as you like, but you can only edit one record at a time. In the tutorial in this chapter, you will use the Edit command to make changes to one of your data records.

Browse

The *Browse command* allows you to edit multiple records in one Browse session. The Browse command will bring up a full screen of records, and you may use the cursor keys to move to fields that you wish to edit and then make your changes. The Browse command is a faster and simpler method of displaying all the records than the Display All command.

Delete

The *Delete command* allows you to mark a record for deletion. You may decide that you want to erase one or more of your database records. The delete command can be used to mark a record with a status of delete. The record is not physically erased with the delete command; it is marked for deletion. If you have used the Delete command to mark a record for deletion; the record will be displayed with an asterisk next to the record. To actually erase a record you must use the Pack command on the database file.

Recall

The *Recall command* can be used to unmark a record that has been marked for deletion with the Delete command. You may decide that you really do not want to delete a particular record, and the Recall command is used to remove the deletion mark from the record.

Pack

If you decide to physically erase the records that you have marked for deletion, you must use the *Pack command.* The Pack command rewrites the database file without the records that are marked for deletion. If you have ten records in your database and you have marked five records for deletion, the Pack command will write out a new file that only contains the five records that are not marked for deletion.

Organize Menu

You will use a second new menu in this chapter called the *Organize Database menu.* The Organize Database menu is illustrated in figure 2.2.

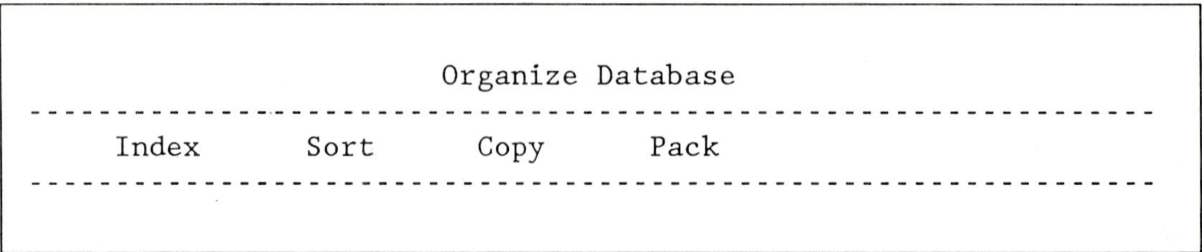

Figure 2.2. The Organize Database Menu.

Sort

You will use the Organize Database menu to *sort,* or put your database file in order by one or more of the fields in the database. You may want to sort your file alphabetically by customer name or numerically by customer number. A database is much more useful to you if it is sorted in order by a particular field. You can then use this organization to find records more easily.

Copy

The Sort command does not allow you to physically reorder the original database file. You must sort the WIDGET file (or any other database file you wish to sort) to another file. You will sort the file WIDGET to a file called TEMP. You can then use the *Copy command* to copy the sorted file, the file TEMP, to the file WIDGET. After you copy the file TEMP to the file WIDGET, the file WIDGET will be sorted in order.

Tutorial Lesson #2

Starting DOS

In this section of the tutorial, you will load DOS into RAM.

1. Put the disk marked "Preboot DISK" in drive A.

2. Put the disk marked "DATA DISK" in drive B.

3. If the computer is turned off, turn it on and go to step 6.

    [This will perform a "cold boot" and load DOS into RAM.]

4. If the computer is turned on, you will hold down the CTRL key, the ALT key, and press the DEL key.

    [This key sequence performs a "warm boot," which reads the DOS program into RAM.]

5. Release the keys.

6. DOS responds with:

    CURRENT DATE IS TUE 1-01-1980

    ENTER NEW DATE:

7. Press: **ENTER key**

8. DOS responds with:

    CURRENT TIME IS 0:01:14:20

    ENTER NEW TIME:

9. Press: **ENTER key**

10.   DOS responds with:

```
THE IBM PERSONAL COMPUTER DOS

VERSION  2.10 (C) COPYRIGHT IBM CORP 1981, 1982, 1983

A>
```

[This is the DOS prompt, indicating that you are in DOS and are logged to drive A.]

Starting dBASE III

In this section of the tutorial, you will load dBASE III into RAM. The dBASE III program will then display the dot prompt.

1.   Place the dBASE III diskette in drive A. Put the Preboot diskette back in its sleeve.

2.   Enter: **dbase**   {press ENTER key}

[This command reads the dBASE III program into RAM. The dot prompt should be displayed at the bottom of the screen. Your screen should match figure 2.3. It will be similar if you are using the educational (DEMO) version.]

```
dBASE III  version 1.00  14 June 1984 IBM/MSDOS ***

COPYRIGHT (c) ASHTON-TATE 1984
AS AN UNPUBLISHED LICENSED PROPRIETARY WORK.
ALL RIGHTS RESERVED.

Use  of  this software and the other materials  contained  in  the
software  package  (the  "Materials")  has been provided  under  a
Software  License  Agreement  (please read in full).  In  summary,
Ashton-Tate  grants you a  paid-up,  non-transferrable,  personal
license  to use the Materials only on a single or subsequent  (but
not  additional) computer terminal for fifty years from  the  time
the sealed diskette has been opened.  You receive the right to use
the Materials,  but you do not become the owner of them.  You may
not alter,  decompile,  or reverse-assemble the software,  and YOU
MAY  NOT  COPY  the Materials.  The Materials  are  protected by
copyright,  trade secrets,  and trademark law,  the  violation  of
which can result in civil damages and criminal prosecution.

dBASE, dBASE III and ASHTON-TATE  are  trademarks of Ashton-Tate.

Press the F1 key for help
Type a command (or ASSIST) and press the return key (↵)
```

Figure 2.3. Initial dBASE III Screen.

Starting Assist

1.   Enter: **assist**   {press ENTER key}

[Loads in the dBASE III assistant program. The dBASE III assistant screen should be displayed. Your screen should match figure 2.4.]

```
The dBASE III
                           Assistant

 Assist uses menus to bring you the power of dBASE III


 -------------------------------------------------------------------
    KEY                          FUNCTION
 -------------------------------------------------------------------
 Esc                     Exit from current operation
 Up arrow                Move to previous menu
 Down arrow              Move to next menu
 Left arrow              Move one item to the left
 Right arrow             Move one item to the right
 Home                    Go to first menu
 End                     Go to right most item
 Option Letter           Executes option (Unless otherwise noted
                         option letter is first letter of option)
 -------------------------------------------------------------------


 Press DOWN ARROW (or ENTER) TO CONTINUE, ESC to EXIT ASSIST:
```

Figure 2.4. Assistant Main Menu.

2.   Press: **ENTER key**

[You have just pressed the ENTER key to continue with the assist program. The Assistant Main Menu is displayed and should match figure 2.5.]

Use Command

dBASE III beeps to tell you that no database is in use. You must either create a new database as you did in chapter 1 or use an existing database. You will utilize the Use command to select the database WIDGET that you created in chapter 1.

1.   Press: **ENTER key**

[You have pressed the ENTER key to select default menu item on the Assist Main Menu, which is the Set Up Environment menu. Your screen should match figure 2.6.]

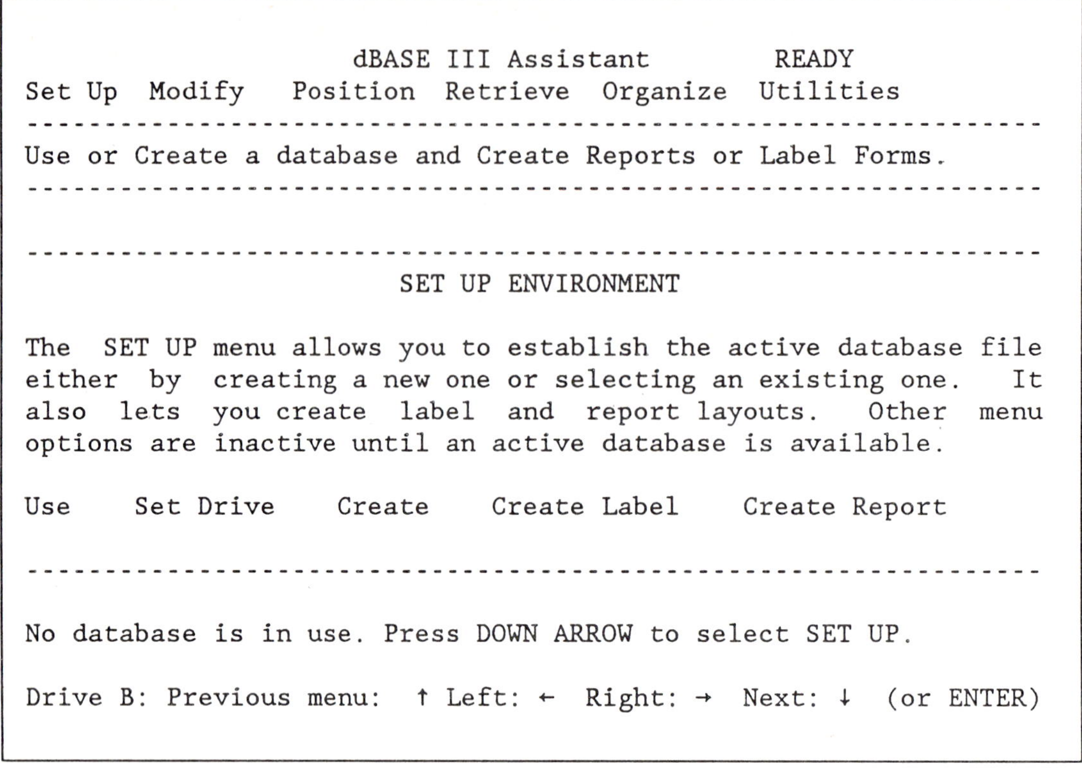

Figure 2.5. Assistant Main Menu.

2. Press: **ENTER key**

[You have pressed the ENTER key to select the Use command. The Use command is the default command on the Set Up Environment menu. This command allows you to select a database as the active database.]

3. dBASE III displays the following prompt:

Press SPACE BAR or arrows to choose disk drive: Press ENTER to select drive.

Disk Drives: A B

4. Press: **ENTER key**

[You have pressed the ENTER key to select the default disk drive of drive B.]

5. dBASE III displays the following prompt:

SELECT FILE—position with ARROW KEYS—ENTER to select—ESC to abort

WIDGET.DBF

6. Press: **ENTER key**

[You have pressed the ENTER key to select WIDGET as your database file.]

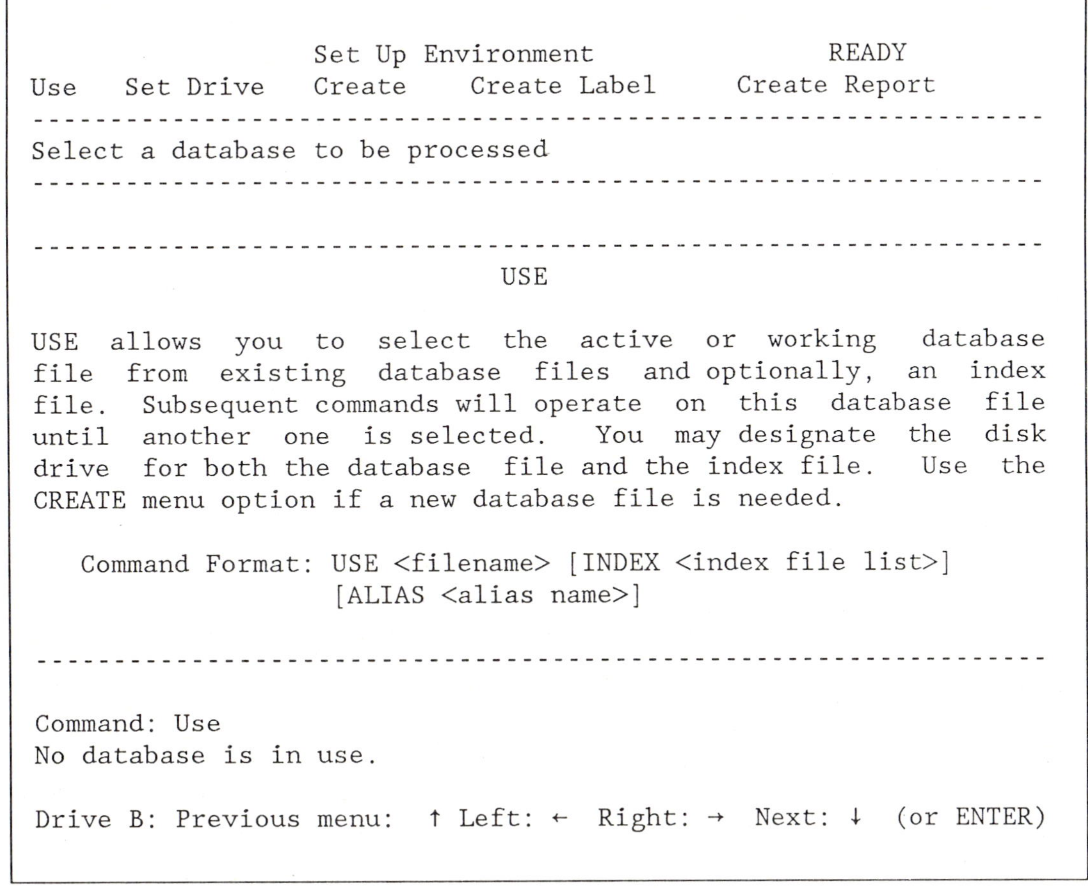

Figure 2.6. Use Screen When No Database File Exists.

7. dBASE III displays the following prompt:

    Is file indexed? (Y/N):

8. Enter: **n**

    [You entered "N" to indicate that the file WIDGET is not indexed. You are returned to the Assistant Main Menu. Your screen should match figure 2.7.]

Add New Records

You are now going to switch to a new menu called the Modify menu. You will then select the Append command from this menu. The Append command allows you to add new records to your database. You are going to add one new record.

1. Press: **RIGHT ARROW once**

    [You have pressed the RIGHT ARROW key once to position the cursor on the MODIFY menu choice. Your screen should match figure 2.8.]

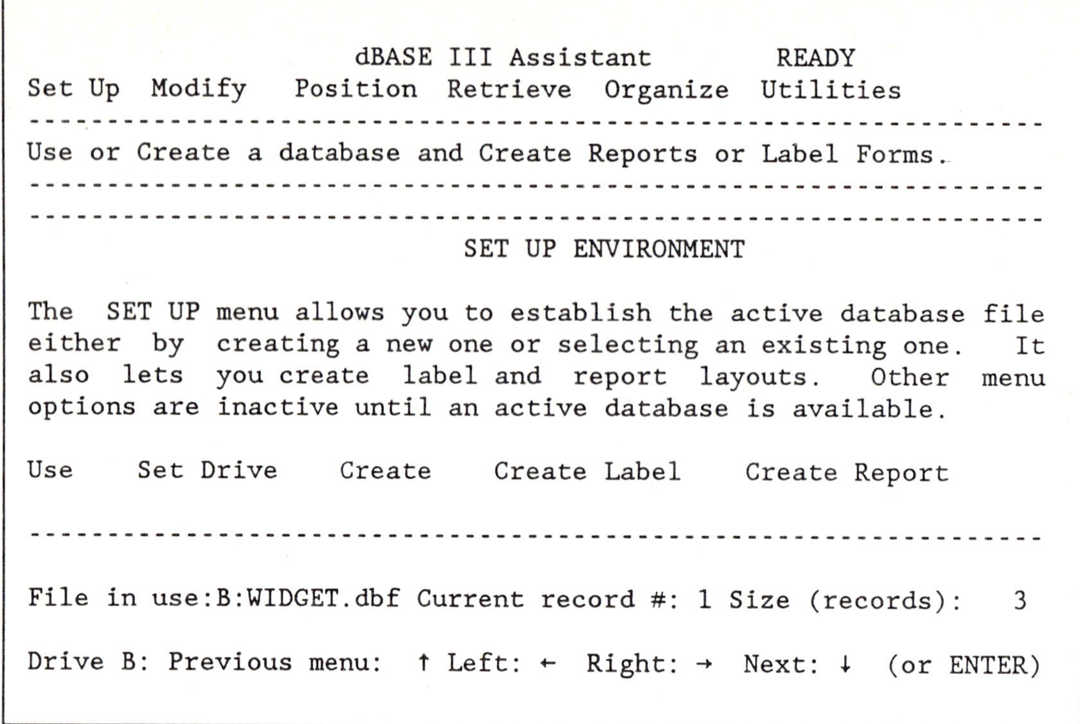

```
                  dBASE III Assistant            READY
Set Up  Modify   Position  Retrieve  Organize  Utilities
--------------------------------------------------------------------
Use or Create a database and Create Reports or Label Forms.
--------------------------------------------------------------------

--------------------------------------------------------------------
                     SET UP ENVIRONMENT

The  SET UP menu allows you to establish the active database file
either  by  creating a new one or selecting an existing one.   It
also  lets  you create  label and  report  layouts.   Other  menu
options are inactive until an active database is available.

Use     Set Drive    Create      Create Label     Create Report

--------------------------------------------------------------------

File in use:B:WIDGET.dbf Current record #: 1 Size (records):   3

Drive B: Previous menu:  ↑ Left: ←  Right: →  Next: ↓  (or ENTER)
```

Figure 2.7. Returned to Assistant Main Menu.

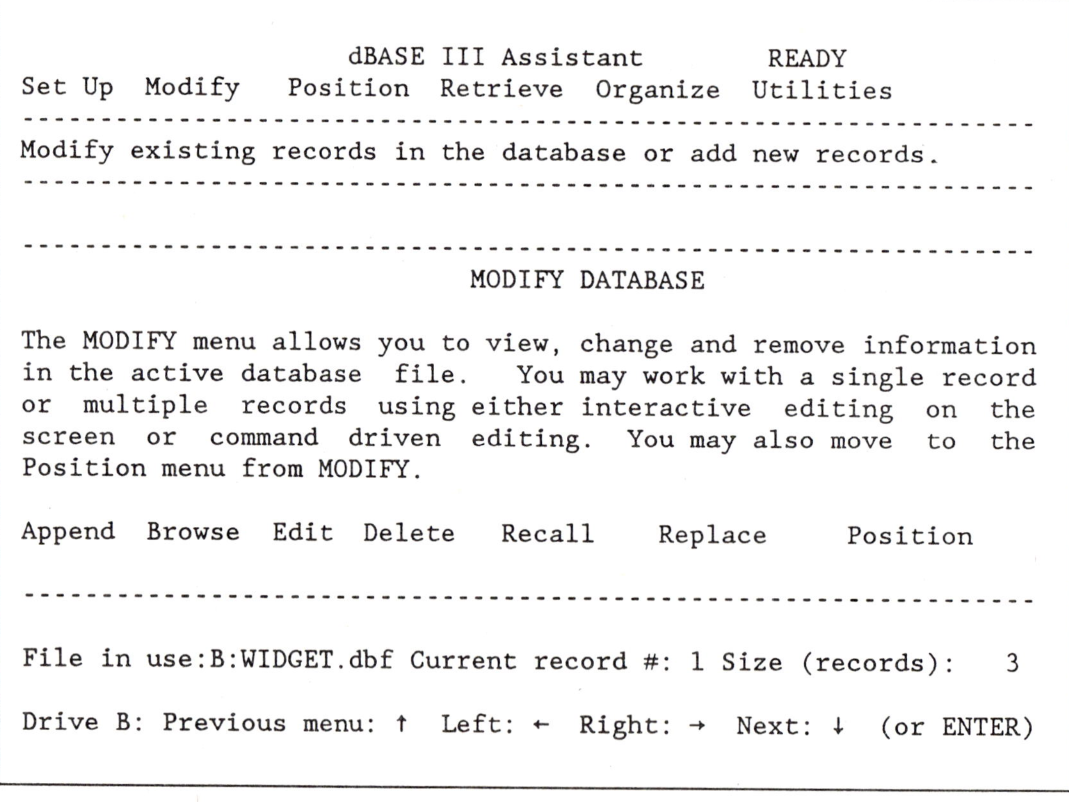

```
                  dBASE III Assistant            READY
Set Up  Modify   Position  Retrieve  Organize  Utilities
--------------------------------------------------------------------
Modify existing records in the database or add new records.
--------------------------------------------------------------------


--------------------------------------------------------------------
                      MODIFY DATABASE

The MODIFY menu allows you to view, change and remove information
in the active database  file.   You may work with a single record
or  multiple  records  using either  interactive  editing  on  the
screen  or  command  driven  editing.  You may also move  to  the
Position menu from MODIFY.

Append  Browse  Edit  Delete  Recall    Replace      Position

--------------------------------------------------------------------

File in use:B:WIDGET.dbf Current record #: 1 Size (records):   3

Drive B: Previous menu: ↑  Left: ←  Right: →  Next: ↓  (or ENTER)
```

Figure 2.8. The Modify Menu.

2. Press: **ENTER key**

[You have pressed the ENTER key to select the MODIFY menu item. Your screen should match figure 2.9.]

```
                          Modify Database                        READY
    Append    Browse    Edit     Delete      Recall    Replace  Position
    - - - - - - - - - - - - - - - - - - - - - - - - - - - - - - - - - - -
    Append records to current database
    - - - - - - - - - - - - - - - - - - - - - - - - - - - - - - - - - - -


    - - - - - - - - - - - - - - - - - - - - - - - - - - - - - - - - - - -
                               APPEND
    Append allows information to be added to the active database file
    using interactive editing on the screen. Information is added one
    record at a time, field by field.

       Command Format: APPEND [BLANK / FROM <filename>
                       [FOR / WHILE <condition>] [SDF / DELIMITED]]


    - - - - - - - - - - - - - - - - - - - - - - - - - - - - - - - - - - -


    Command: Append
    File in use:B:WIDGET.dbf Current record #: 1 Size (records):    3

    Drive B: Previous menu: ↑  Left: ←  Right: →  Next: ↓  (or ENTER)
```

Figure 2.9. The Append Choice.

3. Press: **ENTER key**

[You have pressed the ENTER key to select the default menu item of Append. A data entry screen for record #4 is displayed on your screen.]

4. Enter: **4**   {press **ENTER key**}

[You have pressed 4 to enter this record as customer #4.]

5. Enter: **Bullwinkle Inc.**   {press **ENTER KEY**}

[You have entered the name of the company.]

6. Enter: **78000**   {press **ENTER KEY**}

[You have entered 78000 as the amount owed by Bullwinkle.]

7.   Enter: **^End**

[You have pressed ^END to end the Append mode. You are returned to the Modify menu. Your screen should match figure 2.10.]

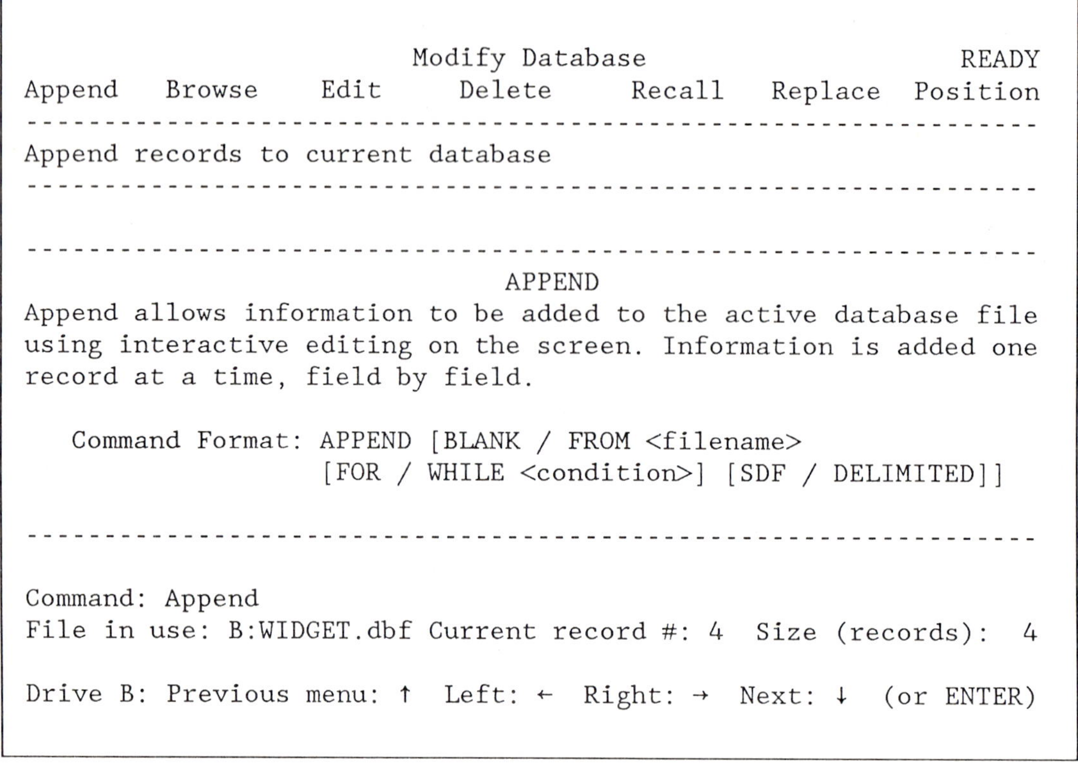

Figure 2.10. Screen After Adding Record #4.

Editing Records

In this section of the tutorial, you are going to learn how to change records that you have already entered. The term *edit* is used in dBASE III to describe the process of changing a record. You will choose the Edit command from the Modify menu and then change a value in a record. The EDIT Command can be used to select one record for editing.

When you have a record on the screen for editing you may use the DOWN ARROW key to move forward, field by field, and you may use the UP ARROW key to move backward, field by field. You may use the PGUP key to move forward one record in the file and you may use the PGDN key to move backward one record in the file.

1.   Press: **RIGHT ARROW twice**

[You have pressed the RIGHT ARROW key twice to position the cursor on the Edit command. Your screen should match figure 2.11.]

```
                         Modify Database                        READY
    Append    Browse    Edit     Delete     Recall   Replace  Position
    - - - - - - - - - - - - - - - - - - - - - - - - - - - - - - - - - - -
    Initiate editing of data in current database
    - - - - - - - - - - - - - - - - - - - - - - - - - - - - - - - - - - -


    - - - - - - - - - - - - - - - - - - - - - - - - - - - - - - - - - - -
                                  EDIT

    The  EDIT  command  allows  interactive  editing  of  a  single  record
    on  the  screen.    The  current  record  is  assumed.    The  POSITION
    menu  may  be  used  to  establish  the  current  record.


      Command Format:   EDIT [[RECORD] <expN>]


    - - - - - - - - - - - - - - - - - - - - - - - - - - - - - - - - - - -


    Command: Edit
    File in use:B:WIDGET.dbf Current record #:4   Size (records):4

    Drive B: Previous menu: ↑  Left: ←  Right: →  Next: ↓  (or ENTER)
```

Figure 2.11. Using the Edit Command.

2.   Press: **ENTER key**

[You have pressed the ENTER key to select the Edit command. Record #4 is displayed. When you use the Edit command, dBASE III always displays the current record.]

Press: **PGUP key**

3.   [You have pressed the PGUP key to move up one record in your database. Record #3 is displayed.]

4.   Press: **PGUP key**

[You have pressed the PGUP key to move up one record in your database. Record #2 is displayed.]

5.   Press: **DOWN ARROW key twice**

[You have pressed the DOWN ARROW key twice to move the cursor to the amount field in record #2. The amount should be displayed as 65000.]

6.   Enter: **75000**   {press ENTER KEY}

[You have entered 75000 in the Amount field for the Al Capone Enterprises record to change or edit the amount from 65000 to 75000.]

7. Press: **PGUP**

[You have pressed PGUP to move back to record #2. Notice that the Amount field now displays 75000.]

8. Press: **^End**

[You have pressed ^END to end the Edit mode and return to the Modify menu. Your screen should match figure 2.12.]

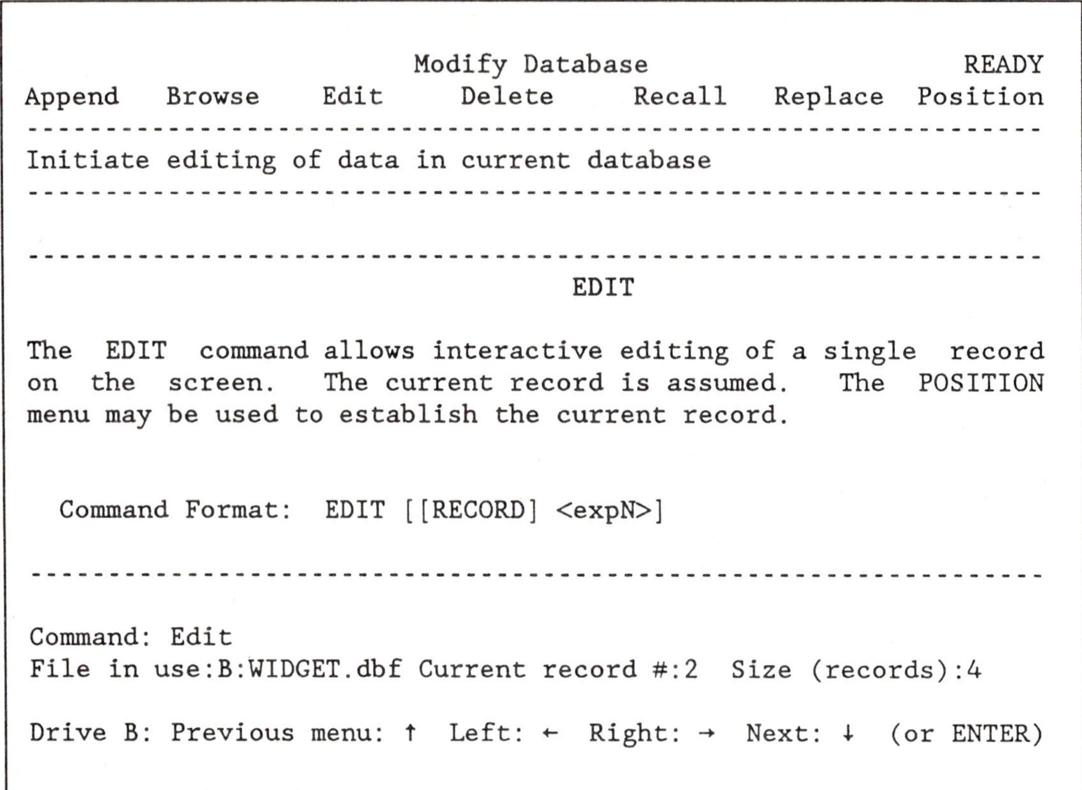

Figure 2.12. Modify Screen After Editing.

Deleting a Record

In this section of the tutorial, you will learn how to delete a record from your database. You begin to delete a record by marking the record for deletion with the Delete command.

1. Press: **RIGHT ARROW key once**

[You have pressed the RIGHT ARROW key once to position the cursor on the Delete command. Your screen should match figure 2.13.]

2. Press: **ENTER key**

[You have pressed the ENTER key to select the Delete command. Your screen should match figure 2.14.]

```
                         Modify Database                        READY
     Append    Browse     Edit     Delete     Recall   Replace  Position
     -------------------------------------------------------------------
     Mark one or more selected records for deletion
     -------------------------------------------------------------------


     -------------------------------------------------------------------
                                    DELETE

     DELETE  allows  records to be marked for deletion,  but does  not
     actually  remove  them.   Records  marked  for  deletion  may  be
     excluded  during  certain  operations,  like  report  generation.
     The  RECALL command is used to reactivate deleted records.   PACK
     is used to permanently remove them.

        Command Format:  DELETE [<scope>] [FOR / WHILE <condition>]

     -------------------------------------------------------------------


     Command: Delete
     File in use:B:WIDGET.dbf Current record #:2  Size (records):4

     Drive B: Previous menu: ↑  Left: ←  Right: →  Next: ↓  (or ENTER)
```

Figure 2.13. The Delete Choice.

3. Press: **DOWN ARROW three times**

    [You have pressed the DOWN ARROW three times to position the cursor on the "Process one specified record" menu item.]

4. Press: **ENTER key**

    [You have pressed the ENTER key to select the "Process one specified record" menu item.]

5. dBASE III displays the following prompt:

    ENTER NUMERIC VALUE:

6. Enter: **4**   {press ENTER KEY}

    [You have entered 4 to indicate that you wish to delete record #4.]

7. Press: **ENTER key**

    [You have pressed the ENTER key to continue with the deletion process.]

8. dBASE III displays the following message:

    1 RECORD DELETED

```
                       Modify Database                        READY
Append     Browse     Edit     Delete       Recall    Replace  Position
- - - - - - - - - - - - - - - - - - - - - - - - - - - - - - - - - - - -
Select scope element
- - - - - - - - - - - - - - - - - - - - - - - - - - - - - - - - - - - -
          - - - - - - - - - - - - - - - - - - - - - - - - - - - - - - -
          :              Process current record (no scope specified)  :
          : NEXT         For the NEXT N records                        :
          : ALL          Process ALL the database records              :
          : RECORD       Process one specified record                  :
          - - - - - - - - - - - - - - - - - - - - - - - - - - - - - - -


Command: Delete
File in use:B:WIDGET.dbf Current record #:2  Size (records):4

Drive B: Press  →  to move to next selection item
```

Figure 2.14. The Delete Screen.

9.   Press: **ENTER key**

[You have pressed the ENTER key to continue. You are returned to the Modify Database Menu. Your screen should match figure 2.15.]

```
                       Modify Database                        READY
Append     Browse     Edit     Delete       Recall    Replace  Position
- - - - - - - - - - - - - - - - - - - - - - - - - - - - - - - - - - - -
Mark one or more selected records for deletion
- - - - - - - - - - - - - - - - - - - - - - - - - - - - - - - - - - - -

- - - - - - - - - - - - - - - - - - - - - - - - - - - - - - - - - - - -
                              DELETE

DELETE  allows  records to be marked for deletion,  but does  not
actually remove them. Records marked for deletion may be excluded
during certain operations, like  report  generation.   The RECALL
command  is  used to reactivate deleted records.  PACK is used to
permanently remove them.

   Command Format:  DELETE [<scope>] [FOR / WHILE <condition>]

- - - - - - - - - - - - - - - - - - - - - - - - - - - - - - - - - - - -

Command: Delete
File in use:B:WIDGET.dbf Current record #:4  Size (records):4

Drive B: Previous menu: ↑  Left: ←  Right: →  Next: ↓  (or ENTER)
```

Figure 2.15. The Delete Choice.

1. Press: **UP ARROW key once**

    [You have pressed the UP ARROW key once to move to the Assistant Main Menu. Your screen should match figure 2.16.]

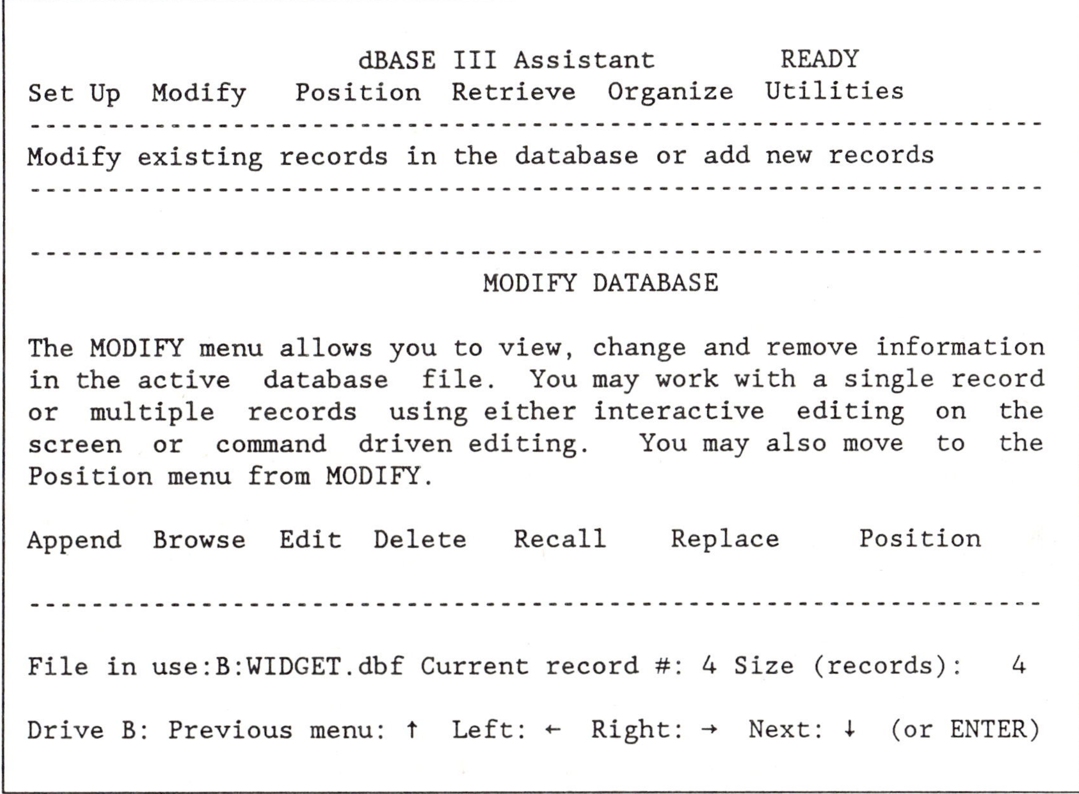

Figure 2.16. Return to Assistant Menu.

2. Press: **r**

    [You have pressed "R" to select the Retrieve menu. Your screen should match figure 2.17.]

3. Press: **ENTER key**

    [You have pressed the ENTER key to select the Display menu item.]

4. Press: **DOWN ARROW key two times**

    [You have pressed the DOWN ARROW key two times to position the cursor on the "Process all the database records" menu choice.]

5. Press: **ENTER key**

    [You have pressed the ENTER key to select the "Process all the records" menu choice.]

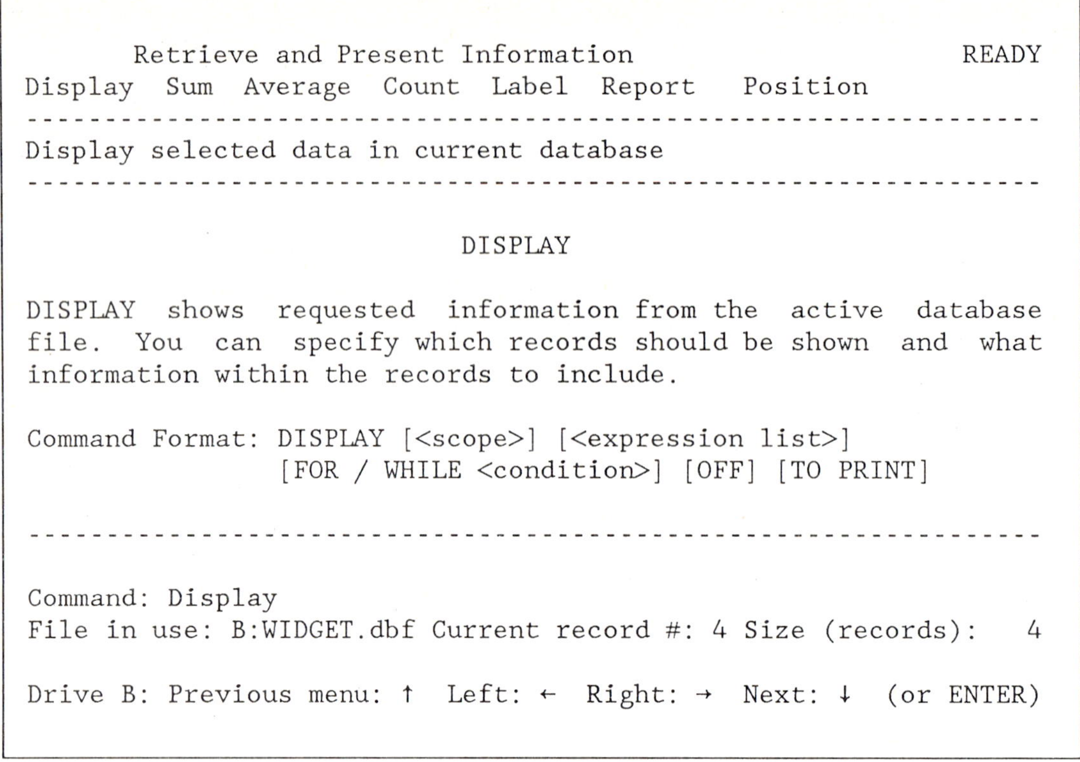

Figure 2.17. The Retrieve Menu.

6. Press: **ENTER key**

[You have pressed the ENTER key to continue.]

7. Press: **ENTER key three times**

[You have pressed the ENTER key three times to mark all three fields for display.]

8. Press: **RIGHT ARROW key once**

[You have pressed the RIGHT ARROW key once to display all the records in your database. Record #4 is displayed with an asterisk to indicate that it is marked for deletion. Your screen should match figure 2.18.]

9. Press: **ENTER key**

[You have pressed the ENTER key to continue.]

10. Press: **UP ARROW key once**

[You have pressed the UP ARROW key to move up to the Assistant Main Menu.]

11. Press: **ENTER key**

[You have pressed the ENTER key to move to the Modify menu.]

```
         Retrieve and Present Information
   Display  Sum  Average  Count  Label  Report   Position
   ------------------------------------------------------------

   Select Field names—Position using ↑/↓ ARROW KEYS—Select using ENTER:
   ------------------------------------------------------------


   Record#  CUST_NUM  CUST_NAME                      AMOUNT
        1  1          Deloren Corporation          9000.00
        2  2          Al Capone Enterprises       75000.00
        3  3          Sidereal Systems            28000.00
        4  *4         Bullwinkle Inc.             78000.00


   Command: Display  ALL   FIELDS CUST_NUM, CUST_NAME, AMOUNT
   File in use:B:WIDGET.dbf Current record#: End of File Size:4

   Drive B:     Press any Character To Continue
```

Figure 2.18. Record Marked for Deletion.

Recall Deleted Record

You may change your mind and decide not to delete a record from your database. You have used the delete command only to mark a record for deletion. You have not yet physically deleted the record. Since you have only marked the record for deletion, you may unmark the record by using the Recall command.

1. Press: **RIGHT ARROW key four times**

    [You have pressed the RIGHT ARROW key four times to move the cursor to menu item Recall. Your screen should match figure 2.19.]

2. Press: **ENTER key**

    [You press the ENTER key to select the Recall command. Your screen should match figure 2.20.]

```
                        Modify Database                          READY
Append      Browse      Edit       Delete       Recall    Replace  Position
-----------------------------------------------------------------------
Reinstate records previously marked for deletion
-----------------------------------------------------------------------


-----------------------------------------------------------------------
                             RECALL

The RECALL command  is used to reactivate records that are marked
for  deletion.   This  command will work on the  entire  database
unless a limiting condition is given. If a PACK command is issued
before using RECALL, the deleted records cannot be restored.

  Command Format:   RECALL [<scope>] [FOR / WHILE <condition>]


-----------------------------------------------------------------------

Command: Recall
File in use:B:WIDGET.dbf Current record:End of File Size (Records):4

Drive B: Press ⟶ to move to next selection item
```

Figure 2.19. The Recall Choice.

```
                        Modify Database
Append      Browse      Edit       Delete      Recall    Replace   Position
-----------------------------------------------------------------------
Select scope element
-----------------------------------------------------------------------
       -----------------------------------------------------------------
       :             Process current record (no scope specified)  :
       : NEXT        For the NEXT N records                       :
       : ALL         Process ALL the database records             :
       : RECORD      Process one specified record                 :
       -----------------------------------------------------------------


Command: Recall
File in use:B:WIDGET.dbf Current record:End of File Size (Records):4

Drive B: Press ⟶ to move to next selection item
```

Figure 2.20. Selecting the Recall Command.

3. Press: **DOWN ARROW key three times**

[You have pressed the DOWN ARROW key three times to position the cursor on the "Process one specified record" menu item.]

4. Press: **ENTER key**

[You have pressed the ENTER key to select the "Process one specified record" menu item.]

5. dBASE III displays the following prompt:

ENTER NUMERIC VALUE:

6. Enter: **4**   {press ENTER key}

[You have entered 4 because you wish to recall record #4.]

7. Press: **ENTER key**

[You have pressed the ENTER key to continue.]

8. dBASE III displays the following message:

1 RECORD RECALLED

9. Press: **ENTER key**

[You have pressed the ENTER key to continue. The Modify Database menu is displayed.]

Browse Command

The Browse command is a quick way to display all database records. You can display all the records faster with the Browse command than you can with the Display All command. The Browse command also gives you the ability to change multiple records. You can only bring up only one record at a time for editing with the Edit command. With the Browse command you can edit many records at the same time.

1. Press: **LEFT ARROW key three times**

[You have pressed the LEFT ARROW key three times to move the cursor to the Browse command. Your screen should match figure 2.21.]

2. Press: **ENTER key**

[You have pressed the ENTER key to select the Browse command.]

3. Press: **PGUP key**

[You have pressed the PGUP key to display all the records. Notice that record #4 is no longer marked for deletion. Your screen should match figure 2.22.]

```
                          Modify Database                      READY
    Append     Browse     Edit      Delete      Recall    Replace  Position
    ------------------------------------------------------------------------
    Perform full screen editing of current database
    ------------------------------------------------------------------------


    ------------------------------------------------------------------------
                              BROWSE

    BROWSE  allows full screen viewing and modification  of  multiple
    records on all, or selected fields.  The BROWSE edit commands are
    displayed at the top of the screen for quick access.

            Command Format: BROWSE [FIELDS <field list>]

    ------------------------------------------------------------------------


    Command: Browse
    File in use:B:WIDGET.dbf Current record #:4  Size (records):4

    Drive B: Previous menu: ↑  Left: ←  Right: →  Next: ↓  (or ENTER)
```

Figure 2.21. The Browse Screen.

```
    Record No.        1    WIDGET
    ------------------------------------------------------------------------
    CURSOR    ←   → :        UP    DOWN  :DELETE        :Insert Mode:  Ins
    Char:  ←   →       :Record:  ↑    ↓    :Char:  Del:Exit:         ^End
    Field: Home End :Page:    PgUp  PgDn :Field:  ^Y:Abort:          Esc
    Pan:              :                  :Record:^U :Set Options:^Home
    ------------------------------------------------------------------------
    CUST_NUM CUST_NAME-------------- AMOUNT-----
    1        Deloren Corporation         9000.00
    2        Al Capone Enterprises      75000.00
    3        Sidereal Systems           28000.00
    4        Bullwinkle Inc.            78000.00
```

Figure 2.22. Screen After Editing with the Browse Command.

4.   Enter: **^End**

[You have entered the ^END command to end the Browse mode. You are returned to the Modify
Database menu.]

Pack Command

You have used the Delete command to mark a record for deletion. You then used the Recall command to unmark the record. You can permanently delete a record so that the record cannot be recalled. To permanently erase a record, you must first use the delete command to mark the record for deletion and then the Pack command to erase the record. The Pack command rewrites the database file excluding the records marked for deletion.

1. Press: **d**

    [You have pressed "D" to select the Delete command. Your screen should match figure 2.23.]

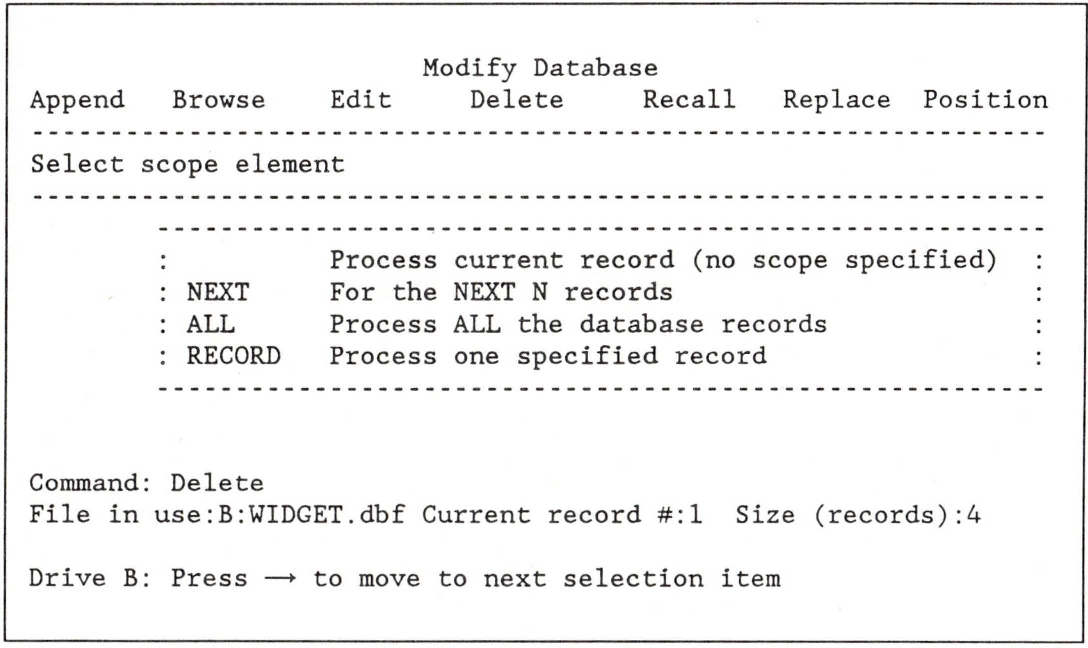

```
                            Modify Database
     Append      Browse      Edit      Delete      Recall    Replace  Position
     ------------------------------------------------------------------------
     Select scope element
     ------------------------------------------------------------------------
              -----------------------------------------------------------
              :               Process current record (no scope specified)  :
              : NEXT          For the NEXT N records                        :
              : ALL           Process ALL the database records             :
              : RECORD        Process one specified record                  :
              -----------------------------------------------------------


     Command: Delete
     File in use:B:WIDGET.dbf Current record #:1  Size (records):4

     Drive B: Press  →  to move to next selection item
```

Figure 2.23. The Delete Choice.

2. Press: **DOWN ARROW key three times**

    [You have pressed the DOWN ARROW key three times to move the cursor to the "Process one specified record" command.]

3. Press: **ENTER key**

    [You have pressed the ENTER key to select the "Process one specified record" command.]

4. dBASE III displays the following prompt:

    ENTER NUMERIC VALUE:

5. Enter: **4**   {press **ENTER key**}

    [You have entered "4" to select record #4 for deletion.]

6.   Press: **ENTER key**

[You have pressed the ENTER key to continue.]

7.   dBASE III displays the following message:

1 RECORD DELETED

8.   Press: **ENTER key**

[You pressed the ENTER key to continue. You are returned to the Modify Database menu.]

9.   Press: **UP ARROW key once**

[You have pressed the UP ARROW key once to move to the Assistant Main Menu.]

10.   Press: **RIGHT ARROW key three times**

[You have pressed the RIGHT ARROW key three times to move the cursor to the Organize Menu. Your screen should match figure 2.24.]

```
                         dBASE III Assistant        READY
      Set Up  Modify   Position  Retrieve  Organize  Utilities
      - - - - - - - - - - - - - - - - - - - - - - - - - - - - - - - - - - - -
      Do operations on the database as a whole
      - - - - - - - - - - - - - - - - - - - - - - - - - - - - - - - - - - - -


      - - - - - - - - - - - - - - - - - - - - - - - - - - - - - - - - - - - -
                            ORGANIZE DATABASE

      The  ORGANIZE  menu  is  used  to  create indexes  for  fast  key
      searches,  sort a database file by field contents,  copy a database
      file and remove information marked for deletion.

      Index             Sort             Copy             Pack

      - - - - - - - - - - - - - - - - - - - - - - - - - - - - - - - - - - -




      File in use: B:WIDGET.dbf Current record #:4 Size (records):    4

      Drive B: Previous menu: ↑  Left: ←  Right: →  Next: ↓  (or ENTER)
```

Figure 2.24. Selecting the Organize Menu.

11.   Press: **ENTER key**

[You have pressed the ENTER key to select the Organize menu.]

12.   Press: **RIGHT ARROW key three times**

[You have pressed the RIGHT ARROW key three times to move the cursor to the Pack menu item. Your screen should match figure 2.25.]

```
                        Organize Database                    READY
     Index             Sort                 Copy             Pack
     - - - - - - - - - - - - - - - - - - - - - - - - - - - - - - - -
     Remove records marked for deletion from database
     - - - - - - - - - - - - - - - - - - - - - - - - - - - - - - - -


     - - - - - - - - - - - - - - - - - - - - - - - - - - - - - - - -
                                PACK

     The PACK command removes all records marked for deletion from the
     database file, but does not reduce its size.   A COPY command   is
     necessary to recover the physical space.

     If an index file is in use, the index file is adjusted accordingly.

                        Command Format: PACK


     - - - - - - - - - - - - - - - - - - - - - - - - - - - - - - - -

     Command: Pack
     File in use: B:WIDGET.dbf Current record #:4 Size (records):4

     Drive B: Previous menu: ↑  Left: ←  Right: →  Next: ↓  (or ENTER)
```

Figure 2.25. Selecting the Pack Command.

13.   Press: **ENTER key**

[You have pressed the ENTER key to select the Pack menu item.]

14.   dBASE III displays the following message:

3 RECORDS COPIED

[dBASE III has created a file that contains only the records not marked for deletion. The message goes by very fast; you may press the ENTER key again to see it.]

15.   Press: **UP ARROW key**

[You have pressed the UP ARROW key to return to the Assistant Main Menu.]

16.   Press: **m**

[You have pressed the "M" key to move to the Modify Database menu.]

17. Press: **b**

[You have pressed "B" to select the Browse menu item. Your screen should match figure 2.26. Notice that Bullwinkle Inc. has been deleted.]

```
Record No.          1       WIDGET
---------------------------------------------------------------
CURSOR  ←   →   :       UP    DOWN  :DELETE       :Insert Mode:  Ins
Char:   ←  →    :       ↑     ↓     :Char:  Del:Exit:           ^End
Field: Home End :Page:  PgUp  PgDn  :Field:  ^Y:Abort:          Esc
Pan:            :                   : Record:^U:Set Options: ^Home
---------------------------------------------------------------
CUST_NUM CUST_NAME--------------- AMOUNT-----
1         Deloren Corporation        9000.00
2         Al Capone Enterprises     75000.00
3         Sidereal Systems          28000.00
```

Figure 2.26. Screen After Deleting Record #4.

18. Press: **^END**

[You have pressed ^END to leave the Browse mode. You are returned to the Modify Database menu.]

Sort the Database

In this section of the tutorial, you will learn how to use the Sort command to put your database in order. You can sort your database in order on any field or fields that you choose. The sort process requires that you sort your database to a temporary output file. At the end of the sorting process you will use the Copy command to copy the temporary file to your original unsorted database file.

1. Press: **UP ARROW key**

[You have pressed the UP ARROW to move to the Assistant Main Menu.]

2. Press: **ENTER key**

[You have pressed the ENTER key to choose the Organize menu.]

3. Press: **RIGHT ARROW key once**

[You have pressed the RIGHT ARROW key once to position the cursor on the Sort menu item. Your screen should match figure 2.27.]

```
                         Organize Database                    READY
-----------------------------------------------------------------
Index              Sort                    Copy              Pack
-----------------------------------------------------------------
Sort records into ascending or descending order
-----------------------------------------------------------------


-----------------------------------------------------------------
                              SORT

SORT allows you to sequence a database file  in  either ascending
or descending order  on one or more  fields.  Sort  physically
reorders  the  database  file while INDEX creates a separate  key
file without changing the database file.   If requested,  case is
ignored  and  a  dictionary  sort  results.  The    "/"  character
preceding the "A",  "D," and "C" without an intervening space is a
part  of  the  command  structure and is typed  as  part  of  the
command.  The "/" character  between "/A" and "/B" indicates  you
must  choose  one  or the other and is not typed as part  of  the
command.

Command Format: SORT TO <new file> ON <field1> [/A / /D [/C]]
  [,<field2>[/A / /D [/C>]],..] [<scope>] [FOR <condition>]
-----------------------------------------------------------------


Command: Sort
File in use: B:WIDGET.dbf Current record #:1 Size (records):3

Drive B: Previous menu: ↑  Left: ←  Right: →  Next: ↓  (or ENTER)
```

Figure 2.27. The Sort Choice.

4.   Press: **ENTER key**

[You have pressed the ENTER key to select the Sort menu item. Your screen should match figure
2.28.]

5.   Press: **DOWN ARROW key once**

[You have pressed the DOWN ARROW key once to select the Customer Name field as your sort field.]

6.   Press: **ENTER key**

[You have pressed the ENTER key to choose the Customer Name field as your sort field. An arrowhead
should appear to the left of the Customer Name field.]

```
                        Organize Database
    Index              Sort                Copy              Pack
    ---------------------------------------------------------------------
    Select field names—Position using ↑/↓ ARROW keys—Select using ENTER
    ---------------------------------------------------------------------


                        Field Name    Field Type    Width   Dec. #
                        CUST_NUM      Character        3
                        CUST_NAME     Character       25
                        AMOUNT        Numeric         11       2




    Command: Sort
    File in use: B:WIDGET.dbf Current record #:1 Size (records):3

    Drive B: Press ⟶ to move to next selection item
```

Figure 2.28. Selecting the Sort Command.

7. Press: **RIGHT ARROW key**

[You have pressed the RIGHT ARROW key to indicate that you have completed choosing your sort fields. Your screen should match figure 2.29.]

8. Enter: **temp**   {press **ENTER key**}

[You have entered the name of TEMP as the file that your sorted file will be sorted to.]

9. Press: **ENTER key**

[You have pressed the ENTER key to continue.]

10. dBASE III will display the following message:

```
     100% Sorted     3 records sorted
```

11. Press: **ENTER key**

[You have pressed the ENTER key to continue. You are returned to the Organize menu.]

```
                        Organize Database
     Index              Sort                    Copy              Pack
     - - - - - - - - - - - - - - - - - - - - - - - - - - - - - - - - - - - -
     Enter DESTINATION filename
     - - - - - - - - - - - - - - - - - - - - - - - - - - - - - - - - - - - -




     - - - - - - - - - - - - - - - - - - - - - - - - - - - - - - - - - - - -
     A filename  can consist of from 1 to 8 letters or digits.  A disk
     drive  letter  (A,B..)  and  a colon  can precede  the  filename.
     Otherwise,  current disk drive is used.      Enter the name of the
     file:
     - - - - - - - - - - - - - - - - - - - - - - - - - - - - - - - - - - - -
     Command: Sort  ON CUST_NAME TO
     File in use: B:WIDGET.dbf Current record #:1 Size (records):3

     Drive B: Press  →  to move to next selection item.
```

Figure 2.29. Choosing Sort Fields.

Copy Command

In this section of the tutorial, you will use the Copy command to copy the sorted data, which is now stored in the file called TEMP, to the original file, which is called WIDGET.

1. Press: **UP ARROW key once**

    [You have pressed the UP ARROW key once to move up to the Assistant Main Menu.]

2. Press: **s**

    [You have pressed "S" to select Set Up from the Assistant Main Menu.]

3. Press: **ENTER key**

    [You have pressed the ENTER key to select the Use menu option.]

4. Press: **ENTER key**

    [You have pressed the ENTER key to select drive B.]

5. Press: **RIGHT ARROW once**

    [You have pressed the RIGHT ARROW once to move the cursor to the TEMP.DBF.]

6. Press: **ENTER key**

[You pressed the ENTER key to select the TEMP.DBF file as the active database file.]

7. dBASE III displays the following prompt:

IS FILE INDEXED (Y/N):

8. Press: **n**

[You have pressed "N" to indicate that the file TEMP.DBF is not indexed.]

9. Press: **ENTER key**

[You have pressed the ENTER key to select the Organize menu.]

10. Press: **RIGHT ARROW twice**

[You have pressed the RIGHT ARROW key twice to position the cursor on the Copy command. Your screen should match figure 2.30.]

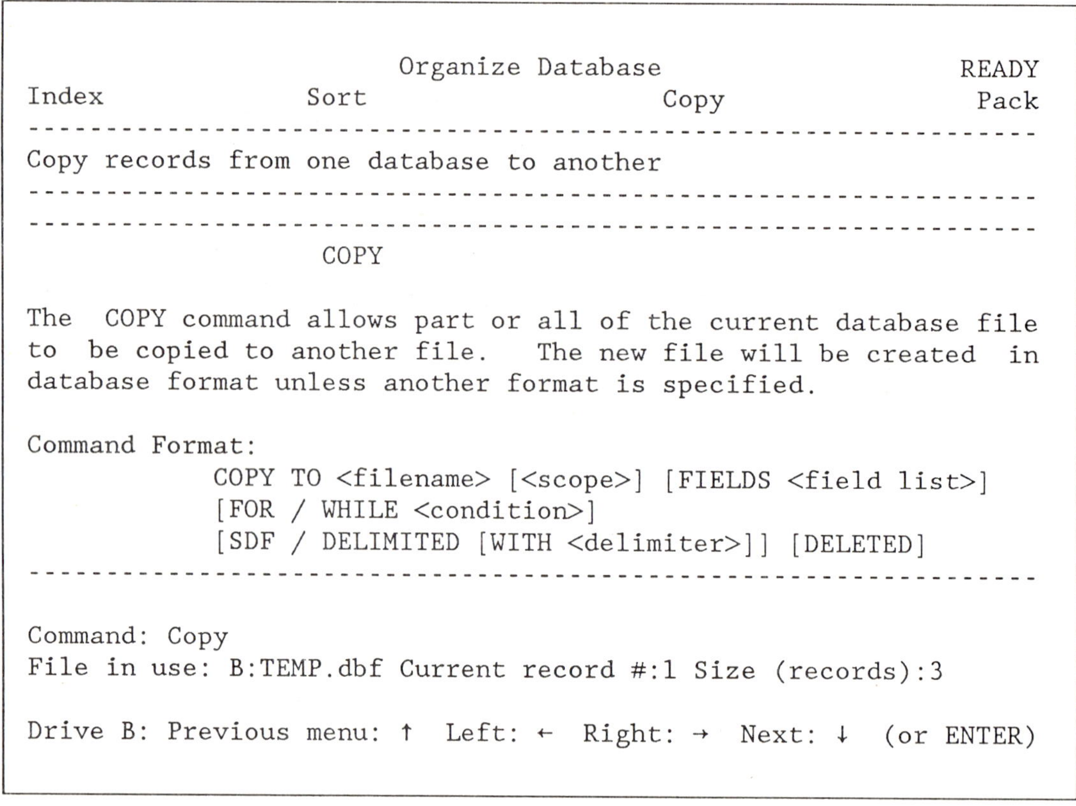

Figure 2.30. Selecting the Copy Command.

11. Press: **ENTER key**

[You have pressed the ENTER key to select the Copy command.]

12.	Press: **ENTER key three times**

[You have pressed the ENTER key three times to select all three fields for the Copy command. An arrowhead should appear to the left of each field as you press ENTER.]

13.	Press: **RIGHT ARROW key once**

[You have pressed the RIGHT ARROW key once to start the Copy command. Your screen should match figure 2.31.]

```
                        Organize Database
-------------------------------------------------------------------
Index             Sort                  Copy               Pack
-------------------------------------------------------------------
Enter DESTINATION filename
-------------------------------------------------------------------




            ---------------------------------------------------
A filename can  consist of from 1 to 8 letters or digits.  A disk
drive  letter  (A,B..)  and  a  colon  can precede  the  filename.
Otherwise,  current disk drive is used.     Enter the name of the
file: [          ]
            ---------------------------------------------------
Command: Copy FIELDS CUST_NUM, CUST_NAME, AMOUNT TO
File in use: B:TEMP.dbf Current record #:1 Size (records):3

Drive B: Press → to move to next selection item
```

Figure 2.31. Copying a File.

14.	Enter: **WIDGET** {press ENTER key]

[You have entered WIDGET as the name of the copied to file.]

15.	Press: **ENTER key**

[You have pressed the ENTER key to continue.]

16.	dBASE III displays the prompt:

WIDGET.DBF FILES EXISTS, OVERWRITE IT (Y/N)

17.   Press: **y**

[You have pressed the "Y" key to overwrite the unsorted WIDGET.DBF file with the sorted TEMP.DBF file.]

18.   dBASE III displays the message:

3 RECORDS COPIED

19.   Press: **ENTER key**

[You have pressed the ENTER key to continue. You are returned to the Organize menu.]

Display Sorted File

In this section of the tutorial, you are going to display the file WIDGET to show that it now contains the sorted data.

1.   Press: **UP ARROW key once**

[You have pressed the UP ARROW key once to move to the Assistant Main Menu.]

2.   Press: **m**

[You have pressed the "M" key to select the Modify Database menu.]

3.   Press: **b**

[You have pressed the "B" key to select the Browse command.]

4.   Press: **PGUP key**

[You have pressed the PGUP key to display all the records. Notice that the WIDGET file is now sorted by name. Your screen should match figure 2.32.]

```
Record No.          1      TEMP
----------------------------------------------------------------------
CURSOR     ←    → :       UP     DOWN  :DELETE       :Insert Mode:  Ins
Char:   ←   →      :        ↑     ↓     :Char:  Del:Exit:          ^End
Field: Home End :Page:   PgUp  PgDn :Field:   ^Y:Abort:           Esc
Pan:                :                   : Record:^U:Set Options: ^Home
----------------------------------------------------------------------
CUST_NUM CUST_NAME--------------- AMOUNT-----
2          Al Capone Enterprises      75000.00
1          Deloren Corporation         9000.00
3          Sidereal Systems           28000.00
```

Figure 2.32. WIDGET File Sorted by Name.

5. Press: **^END**

[You have pressed ^END to leave the Browse mode. You are returned to the Modify Database menu.]

Leaving Assist

1. Press: **UP ARROW key once**

[You have pressed the UP ARROW key once to move up to the Assistant Main Menu.]

2. Press: **UP ARROW key once**

[You have pressed the UP ARROW key once to move to the Assist menu instructions screen.]

3. Press: **ESC key**

[You have pressed the ESC key once to leave Assist.]

Leaving dBASE III

1. Enter: **quit**   {**press ENTER key**}

[You have entered the Quit command to leave dBASE III. You are returned to the DOS prompt. Your screen should match figure 2.33.]

```
 .quit
*** END RUN dBASE III
A>
```

Figure 2.33. Leaving dBASE III.

Commands Summary

Append
: This command allows information to be added to the active database file using interactive editing on the screen. Information is added one record at a time, field by field.

Browse
: This command allows full screen viewing and modification of multiple records on all, or selected, fields. The Browse edit commands are displayed at the top of the screen for quick access.

Copy
: This command allows part or all of the current database file to be copied to another file. The new file will be created in database format unless another format is specified.

Delete   This command allows records to be marked for deletion, but does not actually remove them. Records marked for deletion may be excluded during certain operations, like report generation. The Recall command is used to reactivate deleted records. Pack is used to permanently remove them.

Edit   This command allows interactive editing of a single record on the screen. The current record is assumed.

Recall   This command is used to reactivate records that are marked for deletion. This command will work on the entire database unless a limiting condition is given. If a Pack command is issued before using Recall, the deleted records cannot be restored.

Sort   This command allows you to sequence a database file in either ascending or descending order on one or more fields.

Use   Allows you to select the active or working database file from existing database files and, optionally, an index file. Subsequent commands will operate on this database file until another one is selected.

Review of Menus

Modify Database Menu   `Append  Browse  Edit  Delete  Recall  Replace  Position`
The Modify menu allows you to view, change, and remove information in the active database file. You may work with a single record or multiple records using either interactive editing on the screen or command-driven editing. You may also move to the Position menu from Modify.

Organize Database Menu `Index  Sort  Copy  Pack`
This menu is used to create indexes for fast key searches, sort a database file by field contents, copy a database file, and remove information marked for deletion.

_____ 1. This command allows you to select an active database.
a. Recall   b. Use   c. Browse

_____ 2. This command allows you to unmark records that have been marked for deletion.
a. Recall   b. Use   c. Browse

_____ 3. This command allows full screen viewing and modification of multiple records.
a. Recall   b. Use   c. Browse

_____ 4. This menu is used to sort databases and copy one database to another file.
a. Retrieve   b. Modify   c. Organize

_____ 5. This command is used to write a database to another file.
a. Sort   b. Copy   c. Report

_____ 6. This command is used to put a database in sequence.
a. Sort   b. Copy   c. Report

_____ 7. This command will allow interactive editing of a single record.
a. Display   b. Edit   c. Change

_____ 8. This command allows records to be marked for deletion, but does not actually delete them.
a. Delete   b. Mark   c. Recall

_____ 9. This command permanently erases records that you have marked for deletion.
a. Delete   b. Pack   c. Recall

_____ 10. This command will allow you to add records to the database.
a. Add   b. Modify   c. Append

1. How can you spot deleted records in a display?

2. Once you have used the delete command on a record, can the record be retrieved again?

3. Describe the steps involved in permanently deleting records from your database.

4. Discuss how the Browse command differs from the Edit command.

5. Discuss the process involved in sorting a database file.

Comprehensive Problem

1. Create a dBASE III file called database. The file should contain the following fields:

        FIELD   TYPE   WIDTH
        CUST_NUM   Character   3
        CUST_NAME   Character   20
        STREET   Character   20
        CITY   Character   15
        STATE   Character   2
        ZIP   Character   5

2. Enter the following records into the database:

        Customer number: 1
        Name: Hobbs, Calvin B.
        Street: 18 18th Street
        City: Motown
        State: MI
        Zip: 30056

        Customer number: 2
        Name: Drabble, Norman
        Street: 25 Nowhere Place
        City: Tuleville
        State: CA
        Zip: 10625

        Customer number: 3
        Name: Jones, Spike
        Street: 11 Loretta Lane
        City: Pitsville
        State: PA
        Zip: 90000

3. Use the Browse command to display the database.

4. Press the F1 function key to remove the menu.

5. Your display should match the following:

```
-------------------------------------------------------------------------------------------------
Record No.            1          DATABASE
CUST_NUM   CUST_NAME------------STREET------------CITY---------State---ZIP---
1          Hobbs, Calvin B.     18 18th Street    Motown       MI      30056
2          Drabble, Norman      25 Nowhere Place  Tuleville    CA      10625
3          Jones, Spike         11 Loretta Lane   Pitsville    PA      90000
-------------------------------------------------------------------------------------------------
```

6. Use the DOS print screen command to print the above screen.

    [You must be connected to a printer to use this command. You will use the appropriate command to display the correct screen and then press and hold down the SHIFT key and tap the PRTSC key.]

7.   Use the delete command to delete Spike Jones.

8.   Use the Pack command to rewrite the file without Mr. Jones.

9.   Use the Edit command to change Norman Drabble's record to match the following:

```
Customer number: 2
Name: Drabble, Norman B.
Street: 80 Nowhere Place
City: Tuleville
State: CA
Zip: 10625
```

10.   Use the Browse command to display the database file.

11.   Press the F1 function key to remove the menu.

12.   Your screen should match the following:

```
------------------------------------------------------------------------------------
Record No.           1         DATABASE
CUST_NUM  CUST_NAME------------STREET------------CITY--------State---ZIP---
1         Hobbs, Calvin B.      18 18th Street     Motown      MI       30056
2         Drabble, Norman B.    80 Nowhere Place   Tuleville   CA       10625
------------------------------------------------------------------------------------
```

13.   Use the DOS print screen command to print the above screen.

14.   Turn in both printouts.

3

Using dBASE III at the Dot Prompt

LEARNING OBJECTIVES

After completing chapter three the student will be able to:

1.   Access dBASE III commands at the dot prompt.
2.   Use the Set On command to turn on the data entry menu.
3.   Use the Display All command to display the entire database.
4.   Use the Display All For command to selectively display database records.
5.   Use the Display Record command to display a single database record.
6.   Use the Locate command to find database records.
7.   Understand the difference between the Sort and the Index command.
8.   Use the Index command to reorder database records.
9.   Use the Delete, Recall and Pack commands at the dot prompt.
10.   Use the Erase File command to delete entire files.

THE DOT PROMPT

In this chapter, you will learn how to leave the Assist menus behind and operate dBASE III directly in the *command-driven mode.* You will issue commands at the *dot prompt* rather than choosing the commands from the Assist menus. You will find that you will work more quickly and efficiently in the direct command mode. You will, in many cases, use the same commands as you did with Assist, but you will enter them directly. Several new commands will also be introduced.

ENTER NEW DATA

You will add some new records to your database. To make your job easier, you will issue the *Set Menu On command* to turn on the *Data Entry menu.* The Data Entry menu assists you with the data entry process. If the Set Menu On command is not issued, you would have to work without this valuable menu. To add records to your database, you will use the Append command directly.

Display Command

The *Display command* can be used to display the data records on the screen. The *Display All command* will list all the data records. You may modify the Display All command so that it just lists certain fields within the database.

Display ALL For Command

The *Display ALL For command* can be used to attach criteria to the Display command. For example, DISPLAY ALL FOR AMOUNT> 30000 will list just those records that have an amount greater than 30,000.00.

Locate Command

The *Locate command* can be used to find records. The LOCATE FOR cust_name = "Gumby Ltd." command is used to locate a record when the exact spelling of the data in the Customer Name field is known. dBASE III will return the record number of the record that contains a cust_name of "Gumby Ltd." If, for example, dBASE III returns a record number of 5, you can issue a *Display Record # command* to display this record. The *Locate For "Capone" $Cust_Name command* is used when you do not know the exact spelling of the data in the record in question. This command will locate the record "Al Capone Enterprises" because it contains the string "Capone." If there is more than one record with the same string "Capone" the dBASE III program will find the first one in the file. If this is not the record you want you may enter the CONTINUE command and dBASE III will locate the next record in the file with a matching string.

Index Command

The *Index command* provides a superior way to put a file in order. The *Sort command* introduced in chapter 2 does put the file in order but requires you to also copy the file from the temporary (TEMP) file back to the original file. The Index command allows you to put a file in order without having to create a TEMP file and without having to copy the file from TEMP to the original.

The Index command is also faster than the Sort command. The Sort command manipulates the entire file including all of the fields. The Index command creates a file that contains only the index field and the record number of each record. In the case of the WIDGET file, the Sort command must manipulate three fields and the record number while the Index command only manipulates the index field and the record number.

You can also create as many Index files for a database as you wish. For example, you could have three separate index files for the WIDGET file so that the WIDGET file is in order by cust_num, cust_name, or amount. You should use the Index command rather than the Sort command because the Index command is faster and more versatile.

Edit vs. Browse

The Edit command can only be used to change the values in one record while the Browse record provides a full screen edit. The Browse command allows you to edit a full screen of records at one time.

Using the Delete, Recall, and Pack Commands

You may use the Delete command directly to mark a record for deletion. You can then use the Pack command, which permanently erases all records marked for deletion.

You can use the delete command in a conditional mode. An example would be DELETE ALL FOR AMOUNT > 30000. All records with an amount of greater than 30,000.00 would be marked for deletion. The Recall command can be used to unmark all deleted records at one time. The command to do this operation would be Recall All.

Erase File Command

You may erase from the disk any files that are no longer needed. The command to erase a file called "X" would be ERASE X. The Erase command works on the entire file, not on one record. The Erase command requires you to use the file name and the extension. Database files have an extension of .DBF and index files have an extension of .NDX. If you wanted to erase a database file called X the command would be: erase x.dbf. If you wanted to erase an index file called Y the command would be: erase Y.NDX.

Tutorial Lesson #3

Starting DOS

In this section of the tutorial, you will load DOS into RAM.

1. Put the disk marked "Preboot DISK" in drive A.

2. Put the disk marked "DATA DISK" in drive B.

3. If the computer is turned off, turn it on and go to step 6.

    [This will perform a "cold boot" and load DOS into RAM.]

4. If the computer is turned on, you will hold down the CTRL key, the ALT key, and press the DEL key.

    [This key sequence performs a "warm boot," which reads the DOS program into RAM.]

5. Release the keys.

6. DOS responds with:

    CURRENT DATE IS TUE 1—01—1980

    ENTER NEW DATE:

7. Press: **ENTER key**

8. DOS responds with:

    CURRENT TIME IS 0:01:14:20

    ENTER NEW TIME:

9. Press: **ENTER key**

10. DOS responds with:

    THE IBM PERSONAL COMPUTER DOS

    VERSION 2.10 (C) COPYRIGHT IBM CORP 1981, 1982, 1983

    A>

    [This is the DOS prompt, indicating that you are in DOS and are logged to drive A.]

Starting dBASE III

In this section of the tutorial, you will load dBASE III into RAM. The dBASE III program will then display the dot prompt.

1. Place the dBASE III diskette in drive A. Put the Preboot diskette back in its sleeve.

2. Enter: **dbase**   {press **ENTER** key}

    [This command reads the dBASE III program into RAM. The dot prompt should be displayed at the bottom of the screen. Your screen should match figure 3.1. It will be similar if you are using the educational (DEMO) version.]

```
dBASE III  version 1.00  14 June 1984 IBM/MSDOS ***

COPYRIGHT (c) ASHTON-TATE 1984
AS AN UNPUBLISHED LICENSED PROPRIETARY WORK.
ALL RIGHTS RESERVED.

Use  of  this software and the other materials contained  in  the
software  package  (the "Materials")  has been  provided  under  a
Software  License  Agreement (please read in full).  In  summary,
Ashton-Tate  grants  you a paid-up,  non-transferrable,  personal
license  to use the Materials only on a single or subsequent (but
not  additional) computer terminal for fifty years from the  time
the sealed diskette has been opened. You receive the right to use
the Materials, but you do not become the owner of them.  You  may
not alter,  decompile, or reverse-assemble the software,  and YOU
MAY  NOT  COPY  the  Materials.  The  Materials are protected  by
copyright,  trade secrets, and trademark law,  the  violation  of
which can result in civil damages and criminal prosecution.

dBASE, dBASE III and ASHTON-TATE are  trademarks of Ashton-Tate.

You press the F1 key for help
Type a command (or ASSIST) and press the return key (↵)
```

Figure 3.1. Initial dBASE III Screen.

Add New Data to a File

In this tutorial, you are going to enter dBASE III commands directly at the dot prompt rather than building up the command in the Assist mode. The first command you will enter is the *Clear command*. This command clears the screen. You may enter the Clear command any time you wish to erase what is currently on the screen. You will then issue the Set Menu On command. Assist automatically displays help menus when you are in the Append, Edit or Browse modes. At the dot prompt, you must issue the Set Menu On command to have the help menus displayed in the Append, Edit or Browse modes. You are now going to issue the Append command so that you can add three records to your database. You should examine the help menu when you are entering data. The help menu will tell you what commands and keys you can use to assist you in the data entry process.

1. Enter: **clear**   {press **ENTER** key}

[You have cleared the screen.]

2. Enter: **set menu on**   {press **ENTER** key}

[A menu of commands will be displayed when data is added or edited.]

3. Enter: **use widget**   {press **ENTER** key}

[You have selected WIDGET as the active database.]

4. Enter: **append**   {press **ENTER** key}

[You have entered the Append command, which allows you to add records to your active database. The data entry screen should be displayed and should match figure 3.2.]

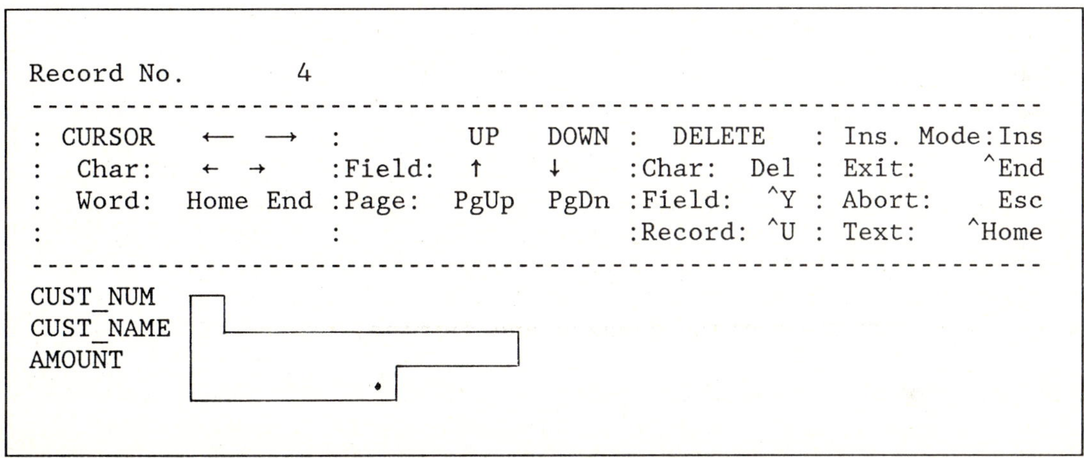

Figure 3.2. The Data Entry Screen.

5. Enter: **4**   {press **ENTER** key}

[You have entered the customer number for record #4.]

6. Enter: **Bullwinkle Inc.**   {press **ENTER** key}

[You have entered the customer name for record #4.]

7. Enter: **78000**   {press **ENTER** key}

[You have entered the amount for record #4.]

8.   Enter: **5**   {press ENTER key}

[You have entered the customer number for record #5.]

9.   Enter: **Gumby Ltd.**   {press ENTER key}

[You have entered the customer name for record #5.]

10. Enter: **35000**   {press ENTER key}

[You have entered the amount for record #5.]

11. Enter: **6**   {press ENTER key}

[You have entered the customer number for record #6.]

12. Enter: **Kickapoo & Sons**   {press ENTER key}

[You have entered the customer name for record #6.]

13. Enter: **54000**   {press ENTER key}

14. Enter: **^END**

[You have entered ^END to end the Append mode. You should be returned to the dot prompt.]

Display Command

You used the Display command extensively in chapter 1. In this chapter, you will use the same Display commands, but you will issue the commands directly at the dot prompt. The first Display command you will use is Display All. The Display All command will list all the database records and will display all the fields. You will then use the Display All command followed by one or more fields. Using the Display All command with selected fields will allow you to display just the fields that you wish to display. Finally you will utilize the Display For command. The Display All For command uses a criteria to selectively display some of the database records. For example, you will use the

```
Display All For Amount > 30000
```

to display just the records that have an amount of greater than 30,000.

1.   Enter: **clear**   {press ENTER key}

[You have just cleared your screen.]

2.   Enter: **display all**   {press ENTER key}

[All the data records are listed on the screen. Your screen should match figure 3.3.]

3.   Enter: **clear**   {press ENTER key}

4.   Enter: **display all cust_name, amount**   {press ENTER key}

[All the data records are listed on the screen. The records are listed without the Customer Number field. Your screen should match figure 3.4.]

```
Record#    CUST_NUM    CUST_NAME                      AMOUNT
      1    2           Al Capone Enterprises       75000.00
      2    1           Deloren Corporation          9000.00
      3    3           Sidereal Systems            28000.00
      4    4           Bullwinkle Inc.             78000.00
      5    5           Gumby Ltd.                  35000.00
      6    6           Kickapoo & Sons             54000.00
```

Figure 3.3. All Data Records Displayed.

```
Record#    CUST_NAME                      AMOUNT
      1    Al Capone Enterprises       75000.00
      2    Deloren Corporation          9000.00
      3    Sidereal Systems            28000.00
      4    Bullwinkle Inc.             78000.00
      5    Gumby Ltd.                  35000.00
      6    Kickapoo & Sons             54000.00
```

Figure 3.4. Display of Customers and Amounts.

5. Enter: **clear**   {press **ENTER** key}

6. Enter: **display all cust_name**   {press **ENTER** key}

[All the data records are listed on the screen. The records are listed with just the Customer Name field. Your screen should match figure 3.5.]

```
Record#    CUST_NAME
      1    Al Capone Enterprises
      2    Deloren Corporation
      3    Sidereal Systems
      4    Bullwinkle Inc.
      5    Gumby Ltd.
      6    Kickapoo & Sons
```

Figure 3.5. Display of Customer Names Only.

7.   Enter: **clear**   {press ENTER key}

8.   Enter: **display all cust_name, cust_num**   {press ENTER key}

[All the data records are listed but the field names are listed in reverse order. Your screen should match figure 3.6.]

```
        Record#   CUST_NAME                    CUST_NUM
              1   Al Capone Enterprises        2
              2   Deloren Corporation          1
              3   Sidereal Systems             3
              4   Bullwinkle Inc.              4
              5   Gumby Ltd.                   5
              6   Kickapoo & Sons              6
```

Figure 3.6. Display with Customer Name and Number Reversed.

Display For Some Criteria

1.   Enter: **clear**   {press ENTER key}

2.   Enter: **display all for amount > 30000**   {press ENTER key}

[Your screen should just display the four records that have an amount greater than 30,000. Your screen should match figure 3.7.]

```
        Record#   CUST_NUM   CUST_NAME                 AMOUNT
              1   2          Al Capone Enterprises     75000.00
              4   4          Bullwinkle Inc.           78000.00
              5   5          Gumby Ltd.                35000.00
              6   6          Kickapoo & Sons           54000.00
```

Figure 3.7. Display of Customers Owing More than 30,000.

3.   Enter: **clear**   {press ENTER key}

4.   Enter: **display all for amount < = 30000**   {press ENTER key}

[Your screen should just display the two records that have an amount less that 30,000. Your screen should match figure 3.8.]

```
Record#   CUST_NUM   CUST_NAME                   AMOUNT
     2    1          Deloren Corporation         9000.00
     3    3          Sidereal Systems           28000.00
```

Figure 3.8. Display of Customers Owing Less than 30,000.

5. Enter: **clear**   {press ENTER key}

6. Enter: **display all for amount > 50000 cust_name, amount**

7. You press: **ENTER key**

[Your screen should display only three records with two fields. Your screen should match figure 3.9.]

```
Record#   CUST_NAME                      AMOUNT
     1    Al Capone Enterprises          75000.00
     4    Bullwinkle Inc.                78000.00
     6    Kickapoo & Sons                54000.00
```

Figure 3.9. Display of Customers Owing More than 50,000.

Locate For Command

The Locate For command is a new command that you can use to find a particular record in your database. There are two versions of the Locate For command. The first version involves a string field in quotes that must match the contents of a field in your database exactly. For example, you will issue the command

```
Locate For cust_name = "Gumby Ltd."
```

Cust_name is a field in your database. You have asked dBASE III to find a record with a cust_name of exactly "Gumby Ltd." If such a record exists, dBASE III will display the record number that contains this cust_name. If the data in the file was entered as "gumby Ltd." or as "Gumby ltd.," dBASE III will not find the record. If dBASE III finds the record, you will use the Display Record # command to display the record.

The second version of the Locate For command will find part of a string. For example, you will issue the command

```
Locate For "Capone" $cust_name.
```

This command will search for the string "Capone" anywhere in the cust_name field. dBASE III will find "Capone" in "Al Capone Enterprises," and it would also find "Capone" in "Joe Capone Inc." You will use this version of the Locate For command when you only know part of the string for which you are searching. If dBASE III finds the string, it will display the record number of the record that contains the string. You will then use the Display Record # command to display the record.

1. Enter: **clear**   {press ENTER key}

[You have cleared the screen.]

2. Enter: **locate for cust_name = "Gumby Ltd."**

3.   Press: **ENTER key**

[You have asked dBASE III to find the record that has a customer name of Gumby Ltd.]

4.   dBASE III responds with the following message:

RECORD = 5

5.   Enter: **display record 5**   {press ENTER key}

[Gumby Ltd.'s record is displayed. Your screen should match figure 3.10.]

```
     Record#   CUST_NUM   CUST_NAME                    AMOUNT
        5       5         Gumby Ltd.                 35000.00
```

Figure 3.10. Using the Locate For Command.

6.   Enter: **locate for "Capone" $cust_name**   {press ENTER key}

[You have asked dBASE III to find a record that contains "Capone" as part of the customer name.]

7.   dBASE III responds with the following message:

RECORD = 1

8.   Enter: **display record 1**   {press ENTER key}

[dBASE III displays the Al Capone Enterprises record. Your screen should match figure 3.11.]

```
     Record#   CUST_NUM   CUST_NAME                    AMOUNT
        1       2         Al Capone Enterprises      75000.00
```

Figure 3.11. Using Locate For to Find a String.

Sort Command

You will use the Sort command to put records in a particular order. If you use the Display All command, the records will be displayed in the order that you entered them. You may find it much more useful to display the records in order by customer name or in order by amount. To display records in a sequence other than the original entry sequence, you must sort the file. The Sort command does not physically reorder the original database file. You must sort the file to a temporary file and then use the Copy command to copy the temporary sorted file to your original database file.

For example, after you issue the command Use WIDGET to make WIDGET the active database file, you will issue the `Sort on cust_num to temp` command. This command copies the database file WIDGET to the file TEMP and then sorts the file TEMP on customer number. You then issue the command Use TEMP to make TEMP the active database. Then you can issue the command Copy to WIDGET to copy the sorted file TEMP to the original file WIDGET. You will end up with a WIDGET file that is sorted in order by customer number.

1. Enter: **clear**   {press ENTER key}

2. Enter: **display all**   {press ENTER key}

[The display should match figure 3.12.]

```
        Record#   CUST_NUM   CUST_NAME                    AMOUNT
              1   2          Al Capone Enterprises       75000.00
              2   1          Deloren Corporation          9000.00
              3   3          Sidereal Systems            28000.00
              4   4          Bullwinkle Inc.             78000.00
              5   5          Gumby Ltd.                  35000.00
              6   6          Kickapoo & Sons             54000.00
```

Figure 3.12 File Before Sorting by Customer Number.

3. Enter: **sort on cust_num to temp**   {press ENTER key}

[The records are sorted in order by cust_num to the file TEMP.]

4. dBASE III displays the following prompt:

    `TEMP.DBF ALREADY EXISTS, OVERWRITE IT (Y/N)`

5. Enter: **y**

[You have entered "Y" to overwrite the file TEMP.DBF.]

6. dBASE III displays the following message:

    100% SORTED   6 RECORDS SORTED

7. Enter: **use temp**   {press ENTER key}

[You have selected the sorted file TEMP as the active database file.]

8. Enter: **display all**   {press ENTER key}

[The display should match figure 3.13. Notice that the records are in order by customer number.]

```
Record#   CUST_NUM   CUST_NAME                   AMOUNT
      1   1          Deloren Corporation        9000.00
      2   2          Al Capone Enterprises     75000.00
      3   3          Sidereal Systems          28000.00
      4   4          Bullwinkle Inc.           78000.00
      5   5          Gumby Ltd.                35000.00
      6   6          Kickapoo & Sons.          54000.00
```

Figure 3.13. File Sorted by Customer Number.

9. Enter: **copy to widget**   {press ENTER key}

10. dBASE III displays the following prompt:

    `WIDGET.DBF ALREADY EXISTS, OVERWRITE IT? (Y/N)`

11. Enter: **y**

    [You have entered "Y" to overwrite the file WIDGET.DBF.]

12. dBASE III displays the following prompt:

    `6 RECORDS COPIED`

Sort Ascending and Descending

dBASE III always sorts a file in ascending order. Ascending order means from low to high. For example, if
you sort a file by amount, the file will be sorted in order from the lowest amount to the highest amount.
You may wish to sort the file in descending order. Descending order is in order from high to low. For
example, you will issue the command sort on amount/d to temp. The /d specifies that you wish to sort from
the highest amount down to the lowest amount. If you do not use the /d parameter, dBASE III will always
do an ascending sort.

1. Enter: **clear**   {press ENTER key}

2. Enter: **use widget**   {press ENTER key}

3. Enter: **display all**   {press ENTER key}

4. The display should match the figure 3.14.

5. Enter: **sort on amount to temp**   {press ENTER key}

6. dBASE III displays the following prompt:

    `TEMP.DBF ALREADY EXISTS, OVERWRITE IT (Y/N)`

```
    Record#   CUST_NUM   CUST_NAME                  AMOUNT
          1   1          Deloren Corporation       9000.00
          2   2          Al Capone Enterprises    75000.00
          3   3          Sidereal Systems         28000.00
          4   4          Bullwinkle Inc.          78000.00
          5   5          Gumby Ltd.               35000.00
          6   6          Kickapoo & Sons.         54000.00
```

Figure 3.14. File Before Sorting by Amount.

7. Enter: **y**

[You have entered "Y' to overwrite the file TEMP.DBF.]

8. Enter: **use temp**   {press ENTER key}

[You have entered the Use command to make TEMP.DBF the active database file.]

9. Enter: **display all**   {press ENTER key}

[Your display should match figure 3.15.]

```
    Record#   CUST_NUM   CUST_NAME                  AMOUNT
          1   1          Deloren Corporation       9000.00
          2   3          Sidereal Systems         28000.00
          3   5          Gumby Ltd.               35000.00
          4   6          Kickapoo & Sons          54000.00
          5   2          Al Capone Enterprises    75000.00
          6   4          Bullwinkle Inc.          78000.00
```

Figure 3.15. Sorting Amount in Ascending Order.

10. Enter: **use widget**   {press ENTER key}

[You have selected WIDGET as the active database file.]

11. Enter: **sort on amount/d to temp**   {press ENTER key}

[You have entered the command to sort the file WIDGET in descending order (high to low) on amount.]

12. dBASE III displays the following prompt:

```
TEMP.DBF FILE ALREADY EXISTS, OVERWRITE IT? (Y/N)
```

13. Enter: **y**

[You have entered "Y" to overwrite the file TEMP.]

14. Enter: **use temp**   {press ENTER key}

15. Enter: **display all**   {press ENTER key}

[Your display should match figure 3.16.]

```
        Record#    CUST_NUM   CUST_NAME                   AMOUNT
             1     4          Bullwinkle Inc.           78000.00
             2     2          Al Capone Enterprises     75000.00
             3     6          Kickapoo & Sons           54000.00
             4     5          Gumby Ltd.                35000.00
             5     3          Sidereal Systems          28000.00
             6     1          Deloren Corporation        9000.00
```

Figure 3.16. File Sorted in Descending Order on Amount.

Index

Using the Sort command to order a file is cumbersome. You must first sort the file to a temporary file and then you must use the Copy command to copy the temporary sorted file back to the original database file. The Sort command is also slow because it has to manipulate all the fields in each record. The Index command is much simpler and solves both of these problems. You just index the original file without having to index to a temporary file. The Index command is also much faster than the Sort command because it creates a separate Index file that contains only the field that you are indexing on and the record number. The Index command does not manipulate all the fields in the database.

For example, you will issue the command Index on cust_name to widname. The Index command creates a separate file called WIDNAME.NDX. This file is used to keep the database file in order by customer name. The WIDNAME.NDX file contains only the Record number and the Customer Name field. You may have several index files for each database file. For example, you are going to create a WIDNAME.NDX file that will order the WIDGET file by customer name, and you will also create a WIDAMT.NDX file that will order the WIDGET file in order by amount. You can then issue the command Use Widget Index Widname to have the file in order by name or issue the command Use Widget Index Widamt to have the file in order by amount.

1. Enter: **clear**   {press ENTER key}

2. Enter: **use widget**   {press ENTER key}

3. Enter: **index on cust_name to widname**   {press ENTER key}

[You have entered the command to create an index file for the file WIDGET. This file will be in order by cust_name.]

4. dBASE III displays the following message:

6 RECORDS INDEXED

5. Enter: **display all**   {press ENTER key}

[The display should match figure 3.17. Notice that the records in the WIDGET file are now in order by customer name. You did not have to use a temporary file to accomplish the index operation.]

```
        Record#    CUST_NUM   CUST_NAME                  AMOUNT
              1    2          Al Capone Enterprises     75000.00
              2    4          Bullwinkle Inc.           78000.00
              3    1          Deloren Corporation        9000.00
              5    5          Gumby Ltd.                35000.00
              6    6          Kickapoo & Sons           54000.00
              4    3          Sidereal Systems          28000.00
```

Figure 3.17. File Indexed by Customer Name.

6. Enter: **index on amount to widamt**   {press ENTER key}

7. dBASE III displays the following message:

6 RECORDS INDEXED

8. Enter: **display all**   {press ENTER key}

[The display should match figure 3.18.]

```
        Record#    CUST_NUM   CUST_NAME                 AMOUNT
              1    1          Deloren Corporation       9000.00
              2    3          Sidereal Systems         28000.00
              3    5          Gumby Ltd.               35000.00
              4    6          Kickapoo & Sons          54000.00
              5    2          Al Capone Enterprises    75000.00
              6    4          Bullwinkle Inc.          78000.00
```

Figure 3.18. File Indexed by Amount.

9. Enter: **use widget index widname**   {press ENTER key}

[You have entered a command to switch your current index file from WIDAMT to WIDNAME.]

10. Enter: **display all**   {press ENTER key}

[Your display should match figure 3.19. Notice that the file is now displayed in order by customer name.]

```
        Record#   CUST_NUM   CUST_NAME                        AMOUNT
              1   2          Al Capone Enterprises          75000.00
              2   4          Bullwinkle Inc.                78000.00
              3   1          Deloren Corporation             9000.00
              5   5          Gumby Ltd.                     35000.00
              6   6          Kickapoo & Sons                54000.00
              4   3          Sidereal Systems               28000.00
```

Figure 3.19. File Indexed by Customer Name.

11. Enter: **use widget index widamt**   {press ENTER key}

[You have entered a command to switch your current index file from WIDNAME to WIDAMT.]

12. Enter: **display all**   {press ENTER key}

[Your display should match figure 3.20. Notice that the file is now displayed in order by amount.]

```
        Record#   CUST_NUM   CUST_NAME                        AMOUNT
              1   1          Deloren Corporation             9000.00
              2   3          Sidereal Systems               28000.00
              3   5          Gumby Ltd.                     35000.00
              4   6          Kickapoo & Sons                54000.00
              5   2          Al Capone Enterprises          75000.00
              6   4          Bullwinkle Inc.                78000.00
```

Figure 3.20. File Index by Amount.

Edit

You have used the Edit and Browse command in chapter 2 in the Assist mode. You will now use the same commands, but you will use them directly at the dot prompt. The Edit command allows you to change the information in one selected record. If you do not know the record number of the record you wish to edit, you may use the Locate For command to find the record number. You will then issue the Edit Record # command to display the record for editing.

1. Enter: **clear**   {press ENTER key}

2. Enter: **use widget**   {press ENTER key}

3. Enter: **locate for "Deloren" $cust_name**   {press ENTER key}

[You have entered a command to find any record that contains "Deloren" as part of the customer name.]

4. dBASE III displays the following message:

RECORD = 1

5. Enter: **edit 1**   {press ENTER key}

[You have entered the command to display record #1 for editing. Your display should match figure 3.21.]

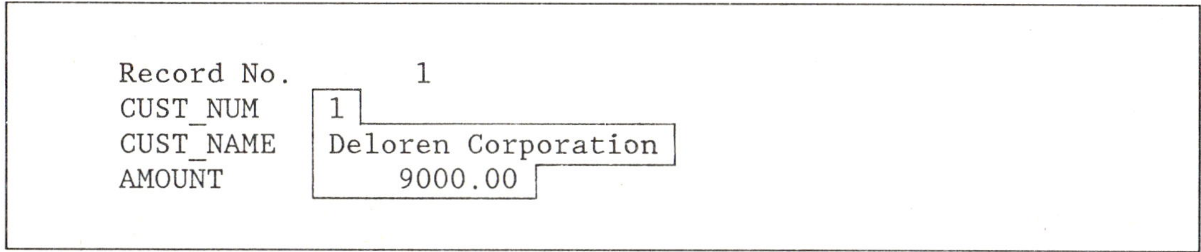

Figure 3.21. Display of Record #1.

6. Press: **DOWN ARROW KEY twice**

[You have pressed the DOWN ARROW key twice to skip to the third field.]

7. Enter: **8500**   {press ENTER key}

[You have changed the amount from 9000 to 8500.]

8. You press: **PGUP key**

[You have pressed the PGUP key to display record #1. Your display should match figure 3.22.]

```
Record No.         1
CUST_NUM    1
CUST_NAME   Deloren Corporation
AMOUNT          8500.00
```

Figure 3.22. Editing the Amount in Record #1.

9.   Press: **^END**

[You have pressed the ^END combination to end the edit.]

Browse

The Browse command allows you to edit a full screen of records at one time. If you want to do extensive editing on the whole file or a portion of the file, you should use the Browse command rather than the Edit command.

1.   Enter: **clear**   {press **ENTER key**}

2.   Enter: **use widget**   {press **ENTER key**}

3.   Enter: **browse**   {press **ENTER key**}

[You have entered the Browse command. This command will display all your database records. Your display should match figure 3.23.]

```
Record No. 1              WIDGET
CUST_NUM   CUST_NAME------------------ AMOUNT--------
1          Deloren Corporation          8500.00
2          Al Capone Enterprises       75000.00
3          Sidereal Systems            28000.00
4          Bullwinkle Inc.             78000.00
5          Gumby Ltd.                  35000.00
6          Kickapoo & Sons             54000.00
```

Figure 3.23. Displaying All Records with the Browse Command.

4.   Press: **END key twice**

[You have pressed the END key twice to move the cursor to the AMOUNT field.]

5.   Enter: **9000**   {press **ENTER key**}

[You have changed the Amount field in the first record of your database from 8500 to 9000. Your display should match figure 3.24.]

```
Record No. 2              WIDGET
CUST_NUM   CUST_NAME------------------ AMOUNT--------
1          Deloren Corporation          9000.00
2          Al Capone Enterprises       75000.00
3          Sidereal Systems            28000.00
4          Bullwinkle Inc.             78000.00
5          Gumby Ltd.                  35000.00
6          Kickapoo & Sons             54000.00
```

Figure 3.24. Changing an Amount in the Browse Command.

6. Press: **^END**

[You have pressed the ^END to end the Browse mode.]

Delete

You have used the Delete, Recall, and Pack commands in the Assist mode. You are now going to issue these commands at the dot prompt. The Delete command does not physically erase a record. The Delete command marks a record as a deleted record. You use the Recall command to unmark a record that you have marked for deletion with the Delete command. The Pack command is used to permanently erase records from your database file. If you have marked records for deletion with the Delete command and you then issue a Pack command, dBASE III will rewrite the file without the records marked for deletion.

You may selectively delete records with the Delete For command. For example, you may wish to delete all records that have an amount of less that 30,000.00. You would simply issue the command

```
Delete For Amount < 30000.
```

dBASE III will mark for deletion all records that have an amount of less than 30000. You will also learn how to use the Recall All command in this section. In chapter 2, you used the Recall Record # command to unmark a particular record. If you wish to unmark all records, you would issue the Recall All command.

1. Enter: **display all**   {press ENTER key}

[Your display should match figure 3.25.]

```
        Record#   CUST_NUM   CUST_NAME              AMOUNT
              1   1          Deloren Corporation    9000.00
              2   2          Al Capone Enterprises  75000.00
              3   3          Sidereal Systems       28000.00
              4   4          Bullwinkle Inc.        78000.00
              5   5          Gumby Ltd.             35000.00
              6   6          Kickapoo & Sons.       54000.00
```

Figure 3.25. File Before Deleting Any Records.

2. Enter: **delete record 6**   {press ENTER key}

[You have entered the command to mark record #6 for deletion.]

3. dBASE III displays the following message:

1 RECORD DELETED

4. Enter: **display all**   {press ENTER key}

[Your display should match figure 3.26. Note that record #6 is marked with an * indicating that this record is marked for deletion.]

```
       Record#   CUST_NUM    CUST_NAME                    AMOUNT
             1   1           Deloren Corporation         9000.00
             2   2           Al Capone Enterprises      75000.00
             3   3           Sidereal Systems           28000.00
             4   4           Bullwinkle Inc.            78000.00
             5   5           Gumby Ltd.                 35000.00
             6  *6           Kickapoo & Sons.           54000.00
```

Figure 3.26. Marking a Record for Deletion.

5.   Enter: **recall record 6**   {press ENTER key}

[You have entered a command that unmarks record #6.]

6.   dBASE III displays the following message:

1 RECORD RECALLED

7.   Enter: **display all**   {press ENTER key}

[Your display should match figure 3.27. Note that no records are marked for deletion.]

```
       Record#   CUST_NUM    CUST_NAME                    AMOUNT
             1   1           Deloren Corporation         9000.00
             2   2           Al Capone Enterprises      75000.00
             3   3           Sidereal Systems           28000.00
             4   4           Bullwinkle Inc.            78000.00
             5   5           Gumby Ltd.                 35000.00
             6   6           Kickapoo & Sons.           54000.00
```

Figure 3.27. Record #6 Recalled.

8.   Enter: **delete record 6**   {press ENTER key}

[You have entered a command that marks record #6 for deletion.]

9.   dBASE III displays the following message:

1 RECORD DELETED

10.   Enter: **pack**   {press ENTER key}

[You have entered a command that tells dBASE III to create a new version of the WIDGET file that
only contains records that are not marked for deletion.]

11. dBASE III displays the following message:

5 RECORDS COPIED

12. Enter: **display all**   {press ENTER key}

[Your display should match figure 3.28. Note that record #6 (Kickapoo & Sons) is gone.]

```
Record#   CUST_NUM   CUST_NAME                AMOUNT
      1   1          Deloren Corporation      9000.00
      2   2          Al Capone Enterprises   75000.00
      3   3          Sidereal Systems        28000.00
      4   4          Bullwinkle Inc.         78000.00
      5   5          Gumby Ltd.              35000.00
```

Figure 3.28. File After Deletion of a Record.

Delete For

1. Enter: **clear**   {press ENTER key}

2. Enter: **delete all for amount < 30000**

[You have entered a command that will mark for deletion all records that have an amount of less than
30000.]

3. dBASE III displays the following message:

2 RECORDS DELETED

4. Enter: **display all for deleted ( )**   {press ENTER key}

[Your display should match figure 3.29.]

```
Record#    CUST_NUM   CUST_NAME              AMOUNT
      1    *1         Deloren Corporation    9000.00
      3    *3         Sidereal Systems      28000.00
```

Figure 3.29. Marking for Deletion Records with Amounts Less than 30000.

5. Enter: **recall all**   {press ENTER key}

[You have entered a command that will recall all records marked for deletion.]

6. dBASE III displays the following message:

    2 RECORDS RECALLED

7. Enter: **display all**   {press ENTER key}

[Your display should match figure 3.30. Note that none of the records are marked for deletion.]

```
        Record#   CUST_NUM   CUST_NAME              AMOUNT
              1   1          Deloren Corporation    9000.00
              2   2          Al Capone Enterprises  75000.00
              3   3          Sidereal Systems       28000.00
              4   4          Bullwinkle Inc.        78000.00
              5   5          Gumby Ltd.             35000.00
```

Figure 3.30. File After Recall of Records Less than 30000.

Erase

The Erase command does not erase a single record, it erases an entire file. You may have a database file or an index file for which you no longer have a use. You can use the Erase command to erase these extra database or index files.

1. Enter: **clear**   {press ENTER key}

2. Enter: **erase temp.dbf**   {press ENTER key}

    [You have entered a command that will erase the entire file called TEMP.DBF. You use this file in your sorting operations.]

3. dBASE III displays the following message:

    FILE HAS BEEN DELETED

4. Enter: **clear**   {press ENTER key}

Leaving dBASE III

1. Enter: **quit**   {press ENTER key}

[Your screen should match figure 3.31.]

```
 .quit
*** END RUN dBase III
A>
```

Figure 3.31. Leaving dBASE III.

Clear	This command clears the screen.
Continue	This command will find the next record that matches the criteria in a Locate command.
Delete For	This command allows you to mark for deletion records that match a particular criteria.
Display All	This command displays all the records in the database with all the fields.
Display All For	This command displays the records that match a particular criteria.
Display Record #	This command displays one particular record.
Erase	This command is used to delete a file.
Index	This command is a faster way to order records than the SORT command.
Locate	This command is used to find data records.
Recall All	This command allows you to unmark all records that are marked for deletion.
Set Menu On	Turns the Data Entry, Edit, and Browse menus on.

_____ 1. This command is used to turn on a data entry menu.
      a. Set Menu Off   b. Set Menu On   c. Display Menu

_____ 2. The dBASE III prompt is?
      a. A>   b. *   c. .

_____ 3. This command is used to display data records.
      a. Locate   b. Display   c. Recall

_____ 4. This command is used to find data records.
      a. Locate   b. Display   c. Recall

_____ 5. This command is used to permanently delete records.
      a. Locate   b. Delete   c. PACK

_____ 6. This command is used to selectively display records.
      a. Locate For   b. Display For   c. Pack For

_____ 7. This command is used to put records in sequence.
      a. Index   b. Erase   c. Recall

_____ 8. This command sorts the file WIDGET in descending order by amount.
      a. Sort . . Amount   b. Sort . . Amount/d   c. Sort

_____ 9. This command is used to delete files.
      a. Index   b. Erase   c. Delete

_____ 10. This command is used to erase the screen.
      a. Pack   b. Erase   c. Clear

1. Discuss the advantages and disadvantages in working directly at the dot prompt rather than with the Assist mode.

2. Discuss the two variants of the Locate command and indicate when each type of Locate command would be used.

3. Discuss the advantages of the Index command over the Sort command.

4. Indicate the commands necessary to sort the file WIDGET by amount first in ascending order and then in descending order.

5. What is the difference between the file WIDGET.DBF and the file WIDGET.NDX.

Comprehensive Problem

1. All of these commands must be used at the dot prompt.

2. Use the file database.

3. Use the Append command to add the following record to your database:

    ```
    Customer number: 3
    Name: Jones, Spike
    Street: 11 Loretta Lane
    City: Pitsville
    State: PA
    Zip: 90000
    ```

4. Use the index command to index the file on cust_name to an index file called name.

5. Use the browse command to display the file on the screen.

6. Press the F1 key to remove the menu.

7. Your screen should match the following:

```
-----------------------------------------------------------------------------------------
Record No.           2           database
CUST_NUM   CUST_NAME------------STREET-------------CITY---------State---ZIP---
2          Drabble, Norman B.     80 Nowhere Place    Tuleville     CA       10625
1          Hobbs, Calvin B.       18 18th Street      Motown        MI       30056
3          Jones, Spike           11 Loretta Lane     Pitsville     PA       90000
-----------------------------------------------------------------------------------------
```

8. Use the SHIFT-PRTSC command to print this screen on the printer.

9. Use the Sort command to sort the file DATABASE to a file called TEMP on zip code in descending order.

10. Use the Browse command to display the TEMP file.

11. Your screen should match the following:

```
-----------------------------------------------------------------------------------------
Record No.           1           temp
CUST_NUM   CUST_NAME------------STREET-------------CITY---------State---ZIP---
3          Jones, Spike           11 Loretta Lane     Pitsville     PA       90000
1          Hobbs, Calvin B.       18 18th Street      Motown        MI       30056
2          Drabble, Norman B.     80 Nowhere Place    Tuleville     CA       10625
-----------------------------------------------------------------------------------------
```

12. Use the SHIFT-PRTSC command to print this screen on the printer.

13. Use the copy command to copy the file TEMP to the file DATABASE.

14. Use the file DATABASE.

15.   Use the Delete command to delete Mr. Jones.

16.   Use the **Pack** command to rewrite the file without Mr. Jones.

17.   Use the Browse command to display the file DATABASE.

18.   Your screen should match the following:

```
- - - - - - - - - - - - - - - - - - - - - - - - - - - - - - - - - - - - - - - - - - - - - - - - - - - - - - - - -
Record No.            1          database
CUST_NUM   CUST_NAME- - - - - - - - - - - - STREET- - - - - - - - - - - - CITY- - - - - - - - -State- - -ZIP- - -
1          Hobbs, Calvin B.        18 18th Street       Motown      MI      30056
2          Drabble, Norman B.      80 Nowhere Place     Tuleville   CA      10625
- - - - - - - - - - - - - - - - - - - - - - - - - - - - - - - - - - - - - - - - - - - - - - - - - - - - - - - - -
```

19.   Use the SHIFT-PRTSC command to print this display on the printer.

20.   Turn in all three printouts.

4

dBASE III at the Dot Prompt, Part 2

LEARNING OBJECTIVES

After completing chapter four the student will be able to:

1. Utilize the Modify Structure command to change the structure of a database. The student will be able to add and delete fields from an existing database.
2. The student will be able to use the Browse command to edit the data in a number of records at one time.
3. The student will be able to use the Home and End keys within the Browse command to move from field to field.
4. The student will be able to utilize the Date field type in a database.
5. The student will be able to utilize the Logical field type in a database field.
6. The student will be able to use the Set command to turn the data entry bell off.
7. The student will be able to use the Sum command to total numeric fields in a database.
8. The student will be able to use the Average command to average numeric fields in a database.
9. The student will be able to use the Count command to display the number of records in a database field.
10. The student will be able to use the Modify Report command to create a report form from a database.
11. The student will be able to use the Report form command to display a report on the screen or on the printer.
12. The student will be able to use the Report Form For command to selectively display information in a report.

MODIFY STRUCTURE

In many cases, you create a database only to discover at a later time that you need to add one or more additional fields to the database. The *Modify Structure command* can be used to add fields to a database. In this chapter, you will add two new fields to your database. You can also use this command to delete fields from your database. The Modify Structure command can also be used to change the size of fields in your database.

DISPLAY STRUCTURE

The *Display Structure command* can be used to display upon the screen the current structure of your database. The structure will show the field names, field types and field widths of all the fields in your database. After you modify the structure of a database it would be wise to use the Display Structure command to make sure that you have made the correct modifications to the database.

Logical Field Type

In chapter 1, when you originally created the database WIDGET, you used two types of fields. The two field types were character, represented by the Customer Name field, and the numeric field type, represented by the Amount field. In this chapter, you will add the Overdue field to indicate if a record is overdue or not. The Overdue field represents a new type of field, the *logical field type*. This type of field only has two possible entries "Y" or "N". You can use the true or false nature of the field to selectively print out reports on your database. For example, you could print out a report for just those records that are overdue.

Date Field Type

The second new field that you will add is a *date field type*. This is a special type of field that contains a date in the mm/dd/yy format. dBASE III has a number of date functions and commands that can be used to manipulate date type fields.

Set Bell Off

When you are entering data, a bell will ring whenever you reach the end of a field. This bell can become an irritant. You can use the *Set Bell Off command* to turn off the sound of this bell.

NUMERIC MANIPULATION COMMANDS

Several numeric manipulation commands are introduced in this chapter.

Sum

The *Sum command* can be used to total a field without creating a complete report. The Sum Amount command could be used to get a quick total of the amount field. The Sum Amount For Overdue command can be used to get a quick total of just the overdue amounts.

Average

The *Average command* can be used to get a quick average of any numeric field. The Average Amount command will give us a display of the average amount. An average is often called an arithmetic mean.

Count

The *Count command* can be used to generate a count of the number of any numeric field. The Count For Overdue command will give a display of the number of overdue amounts. The Count command also tells you how many records you have in your database file.

Modify Report

The *Modify Report command* is used to create a report layout and save the layout on disk. The headings and the margins are entered first. The fields that are to be included on the report are then entered. You may use the Modify Report command to create a new report, or you may use this command to change an existing report.

Report Form

The *Report Form command* is used to display the report created by the Modify Report command on the screen. A selective report may be generated by issuing the *Report Form For command*. For example, the Report Form For Overdue command will list just those records that are overdue.

Report Form to Print

The *Report Form to Print command* may be used to put the report out on the printer rather than on the screen.

Tutorial Lesson #4

Starting DOS

In this section of the tutorial you will load DOS into RAM.

1. Put the disk marked "Preboot DISK" in drive A.

2. Put the disk marked "DATA DISK" in drive B.

3. If the computer is turned off, turn it on and go to step 6.

    [This will perform a "cold boot" and load DOS into RAM.]

4. If the computer is turned on, you will hold down the CTRL key, the ALT key, and press the DEL key.

    [This key sequence performs a "warm boot," which reads the DOS program into RAM.]

5. Release the keys.

6. DOS responds with:

    CURRENT DATE IS TUE 1—01—1980

    ENTER NEW DATE:

7. Press: **ENTER key**

8. DOS responds with:

    CURRENT TIME IS 0:01:14:20

    ENTER NEW TIME:

9. Press: **ENTER key**

10. DOS responds with:

    THE IBM PERSONAL COMPUTER DOS

    VERSION 2.10 (C) COPYRIGHT IBM CORP 1981, 1982, 1983

    A>

    [This is the DOS prompt, indicating that you are in DOS and are logged to drive A.]

Starting dBASE III

In this section of the tutorial, you will load dBASE III into RAM. The dBASE III program will then display the dot prompt.

1. Place the dBASE III diskette in drive A. Put the Preboot diskette back in its sleeve.

2. Enter: **dBASE III**   {press **ENTER key**}

    [This command reads the dBASE III program into RAM. The dot prompt should be displayed at the bottom of the screen. Your screen should match figure 4.1. It will be similar if you are using the educational (DEMO) version.]

Modify Structure

You are now going to learn how to use the Modify Structure command to change the structure of your database. The structure of the database WIDGET was originally designed in chapter 1 when you used the Create command. The structure is the field names, field types, and field widths that make up your database. In many cases, you will find that you need to add fields to your database.

In this section of the tutorial, you are going to add two new fields to your database. You are going to add a field called "overdue." This Overdue field represents a new field type called the logical field type. A logical field type has only two possible data entries, "Y" for yes and "N" for no. If the Overdue field in a record contained a "Y", that record is overdue.

You are also going to add a field called "date" to your database. This field also represents a new type of field called a Date field. A Date field contains information in the mm/dd/yy format. This Date field will represent the last date that this record had a payment recorded.

1. Enter: **clear**   {press **ENTER key**}

2. Enter: **set menu on**   {press **ENTER key**}

    [You have entered the Set Menu On command to display the help menus in the Modify Structure and Browse modes.]

```
dBASE III  version 1.00  14 June 1984 IBM/MSDOS ***

COPYRIGHT (c) ASHTON-TATE 1984
AS AN UNPUBLISHED LICENSED PROPRIETARY WORK.
ALL RIGHTS RESERVED.

Use  of  this software and the other materials contained  in  the
software  package  (the "Materials")  has been provided  under  a
Software  License  Agreement (please read in full).  In  summary,
Ashton-Tate  grants  you a paid-up,  non-transferrable,  personal
license to use the Materials only on a single or subsequent  (but
not additional)  computer terminal for fifty years from the  time
the sealed diskette has been opened. You receive the right to use
the Materials, but you do not become the owner of them.  You  may
not  alter,  decompile, or reverse-assemble the software, and YOU
MAY  NOT  COPY  the  Materials.  The Materials are  protected  by
copyright,  trade secrets, and trademark law,  the  violation  of
which can result in civil damages and criminal prosecution.

dBASE, dBASE III and ASHTON-TATE are trademarks of Ashton-Tate.

You press: the F1 key for help
Type a command (or ASSIST) and press the return key (↵)
```

Figure 4.1. Initial dBASE III Screen.

3. **Enter: use widget**   {press ENTER key}

[Makes WIDGET.DBF your active database file.]

4. **Enter: modify structure**   {press ENTER key}

[Your screen should display the current structure of the database. Your screen should match figure 4.2.]

5. Press: **DOWN ARROW key three times**

[You have just moved the cursor to a new field.]

6. **Enter: overdue**   {press ENTER key}

[You have added a new field called the Overdue field to your database.]

7. Enter: **L**

[You have declared the Overdue field to be a logical type of field.]

```
    B:widget.dbf                              Bytes remaining:   3961
                                              Fields defined:       3


    --------------------------------------------------------------
    : CURSOR    ←   →   :           UP    DOWN : DELETE    : Ins. Mode:Ins
    :  Char:    ←   →    :Field:    ↑     ↓    :Char:  Del : Exit:    ^End
    :  Word:  Home End  :Page:   PgUp  PgDn :Field:  ^Y : Abort:    Esc
    :  Pan    ^←   ^→   :                    :Record: ^U : Text:   ^Home
    --------------------------------------------------------------

            field name   type      width  dec
         --------------------------------
      1  CUST_NUM    Char/text     3
      2  CUST_NAME   Char/text    25
      3  AMOUNT      Numeric      11     2






    Names start with a letter; the remainder may be letters,
    digits, or underscore.
```

Figure 4.2. Current Structure of the Database.

8. **Enter: date**   {**press ENTER key**}

[You have added a second new field called the Date field to your database.]

9. **Enter: d**

[You have declared the Date field to be a date type of field.]

10. **Press: ^END**

[You have pressed ^END to exit the Modify Structure command.]

11. dBASE III displays the following prompt:

DATABASE RECORDS WILL BE APPENDED FROM BACKUP FIELDS OF THE SAME NAME ONLY!!

HIT RETURN TO CONFIRM--OR ANY OTHER KEY TO RESUME

12. **Press: ENTER key**

[You have pressed the ENTER key to continue.]

13.   Enter: **modify structure**   {press ENTER key}

[Your screen should match figure 4.3.]

```
  B:widget.dbf                        Bytes remaining:    3952
                                      Fields defined:        5


  ----------------------------------------------------------------
  : CURSOR    ←   →   :          UP   DOWN :  DELETE    : Ins. Mode:Ins
  :  Char:    ←   →   :Field:    ↑    ↓    :Char:  Del : Exit:      ^End
  :  Word:  Home End :Page:   PgUp PgDn :Field:   ^Y : Abort:     Esc
  :  Pan     ^←   ^→   :                  :Record: ^U : Text:     ^Home
  ----------------------------------------------------------------


        field name    type        width  dec
        ----------------------------------------
    1   CUST_NUM      Char/text      3
    2   CUST_NAME     Char/text     25
    3   AMOUNT        Numeric       11      2
    4   OVERDUE       Logical        1
    5   DATE          Date           8




  Names start with a letter; the remainder may be letters,
  digits, or underscore
```

Figure 4.3. Modified Structure of the Database.

14.   Press: **ESC key**

[You have pressed the ESC key to leave the Modify Structure mode.]

Adding New Data

You have now added two fields to each record in your database, the Overdue field and the Date field. You now have to enter data into these fields. The fields exist in each record, but they contain no data. You are going to use the Browse command to add the new data. The Browse command displays the entire record on the screen and allows you to change any field in any record.

1.   Enter: **use widget**   {press ENTER key}

2. Enter: **browse**   {press ENTER key}

[This command will allow you to put data in your new fields. All the records and all the fields in your database should be displayed upon the screen. Your screen should match figure 4.4.]

```
Record No.         1     widget
--------------------------------------------------------------
: CURSOR    ←   →   :      UP   DOWN :  DELETE    : Ins. Mode:Ins
:  Char:    ←   →   :Field:   ↑    ↓   :Char:  Del : Exit:     ^End
:  Word:  Home End :Page:  PgUp PgDn :Field:  ^Y : Abort:    Esc
:  Pan     ^←   ^→   :                 :Record: ^U : Text:   ^Home
--------------------------------------------------------------
CUST_NUM CUST_NAME----------- AMOUNT-----  OVERDUE DATE---
1          Deloren Corporation    9000.00 ?        /  /
2          Al Capone Enterprises 75000.00 ?        /  /
3          Sidereal Systems      28000.00 ?        /  /
4          Bullwinkle Inc.       78000.00 ?        /  /
5          Gumby Ltd.            35000.00 ?        /  /
```

Figure 4.4.

3. Press: **END key three times**

[You have pressed the END key three times to move the cursor to the Overdue field.]

4. Enter: **n**

[You have entered a "N" to indicate that this record is not overdue.]

5. Enter: **031085**

[You have entered a date of 03/10/85 in the Date field.]

6. Press: **HOME key**

[You have pressed the HOME key to move the cursor into the Overdue field.]

7. Enter: **y**

[You have entered a "Y" to indicate that this record is overdue.]

8. Enter: **021085**

[You have entered a date of 02/10/85 in the Date field.]

9. Press: **^END**

[You have pressed ^END to exit the Browse mode.]

Isn't that bell an irritant? We can turn that crummy bell off!

1. **Enter: set bell off**   {press **ENTER** key}

   [You have entered the Set Bell Off command to turn off the data entry bell that will ring as you reach the end of each field.]

2. **Enter: browse**   {press **ENTER** key}

   [Your screen should match figure 4.5.]

```
Record No.         3      widget
---------------------------------------------------------------
: CURSOR    ←  →  :          UP    DOWN :  DELETE    : Ins. Mode:Ins
:  Char:    ←  →  :Field:    ↑     ↓      :Char:  Del : Exit:     ^End
:  Word:  Home End :Page:  PgUp  PgDn :Field:  ^Y : Abort:    Esc
:  Pan     ^←   ^→  :                   :Record: ^U : Text:    ^Home
---------------------------------------------------------------
CUST_NUM CUST_NAME----------- AMOUNT----- OVERDUE DATE---
3          Sidereal Systems     28000.00 ?        /  /
4          Bullwinkle Inc.      78000.00 ?        /  /
5          Gumby Ltd.           35000.00 ?        /  /
```

Figure 4.5. Database in Browse Mode.

3. **Press: END key three times**

   [You have pressed the END key three times to move the cursor into the Overdue field.]

4. **Enter: n**

   [You have entered a "N" to indicate that this record is not overdue.]

5. **Enter: 031585**

   [You have entered a date of 03/15/85 in the Date field.]

6. **Press: HOME key**

   [You have pressed the HOME key to move the cursor into the Overdue field.]

7. **Enter: y**

   [You have entered a "Y" to indicate that this record is overdue.]

8.   Enter: **021085**

[You have entered a date of 02/10/85 in the Date field.]

9.   Press: **HOME key**

[You have pressed the HOME key to move the cursor into the Overdue field.]

10.   Enter: **n**

[You have entered a "N" to indicate that this record is not overdue.]

11.   Enter: **032085**

[You have entered a date of 03/20/85 in the Date field.]

12.   dBASE III displays the following prompt at the top of the screen:

→ ADD NEW RECORDS? (Y/N)

13.   Enter: **n**

[You have pressed "N" to indicate that you do not wish to add any new records.]

14.   Press: **^END**

[You have pressed ^END to end the Browse mode.]

15.   Enter: **display all**   {press ENTER key}

[Your screen should match figure 4.6.]

```
CUST_NUM   CUST_NAME                AMOUNT OVERDUE DATE
1          Deloren Corporation      9000.00 .F.        03/10/85
2          Al Capone Enterprises   75000.00 .T.        02/10/85
3          Sidereal Systems        28000.00 .F.        03/15/85
4          Bullwinkle Inc.         78000.00 .T.        02/10/85
5          Gumby Ltd.              35000.00 .F.        03/20/85
```

Figure 4.6. File After Addition of Two New Records.

[You entered "Y" for "Yes" and "N" for "No." dBASE III displays .T for "Yes" and .F for "No."]

Numeric Commands

The numeric commands are used to give you quick snapshots of what is contained in the database. For
example, if you wanted to know what is the total amount owed you at this time, you can use the Sum
command to total the Amount field. You can also use the Average command to find the average size of any
numeric field. You can use the Count command to find out how many records are contained within your

database. The Sum or Count command can be combined with the Overdue logical field to extract the number of overdue accounts or the total amount owed by the overdue accounts.

Sum

1. Enter: **clear**   {press ENTER key}

2. Enter: **use widget**   {press ENTER key}

3. Enter: **sum amount**   {press ENTER key}

[You have asked dBASE III to total the Amount field for all the records in the database. Your screen should match figure 4.7.]

```
    5 records summed
       amount
    225000.00
```

Figure 4.7. Summing the Amount Field.

4. Enter: **sum amount for overdue**   {press ENTER key}

[You have asked dBASE III to total the Amount field for just those records that are overdue. Your screen should match figure 4.8.]

```
    2 records summed
       amount
    153000.00
```

Figure 4.8. Summing Two Records.

Average

1. Enter: **average amount**   {press ENTER key}

[You have asked dBASE III to compute the average amount owed for all of the database records. Your screen should match figure 4.9.]

```
    5 records averaged
       amount
    45000.00
```

Figure 4.9. Averaging the Amount Field for File Records.

2. Enter: **average for overdue**   {press ENTER key}

[You have asked dBASE III to compute the average amount owed by just those records that are overdue. Your screen should match figure 4.10.]

```
    2 records averaged
       amount
    76500.00
```

Figure 4.10. Averaging the Amount Overdue Records.

Count

1. Enter: **count**   {press ENTER key}

    [dBASE III responds with 5 records.]

2. Enter: **count for overdue**   {press ENTER key}

    [dBASE III responds with 2 records.]

3. Enter: **count for .not. overdue**   {press ENTER key}

    [dBASE III responds with 3 records.]

Modify Report

You can use the numeric manipulation commands Sum, Average, and Count to get quick summaries of the information that is in your database. You often need to have a more complete listing of what is contained in your database. The Modify Report command can be used to create reports that can be displayed on the screen or printed out on your printer. You can put any field that you want on a report. You can create a report that has the fields displayed or printed in a different order than the fields are structured in the database. For example, you could have a report that prints the customer name before it prints the customer number.

You can use different indexes and print or display reports in order by customer name or in order by amount. You simply choose the index that you want to use and then print or display your report. The Modify Report command displays several screens for you that allow you to select report headings, margins and fields, and field headers. You may choose to have a numeric field totaled on your report. The report is saved on disk so that you may use the Modify Report command to change the report at a future date.

1. Enter: **clear**   {press ENTER key}

2. Enter: **use widget**   {press ENTER key}

3. Enter: **index on cust_name to widname**   {press ENTER key}

[You have entered the command to put the WIDGET file in order by customer name.]

4.   dBASE III displays the following prompt:

```
WIDNAME.NDX ALREADY EXISTS, OVERWRITE IT? (Y/N)
```

5.   Enter: **y**

[You have entered "Y" to overwrite the old index file.]

6.   Enter: **modify report acctlist**   {**press ENTER key**}

[The first page of the Report questionnaire is displayed.]

7.   Press: **Function key F1**

[Your screen should match figure 4.11.]

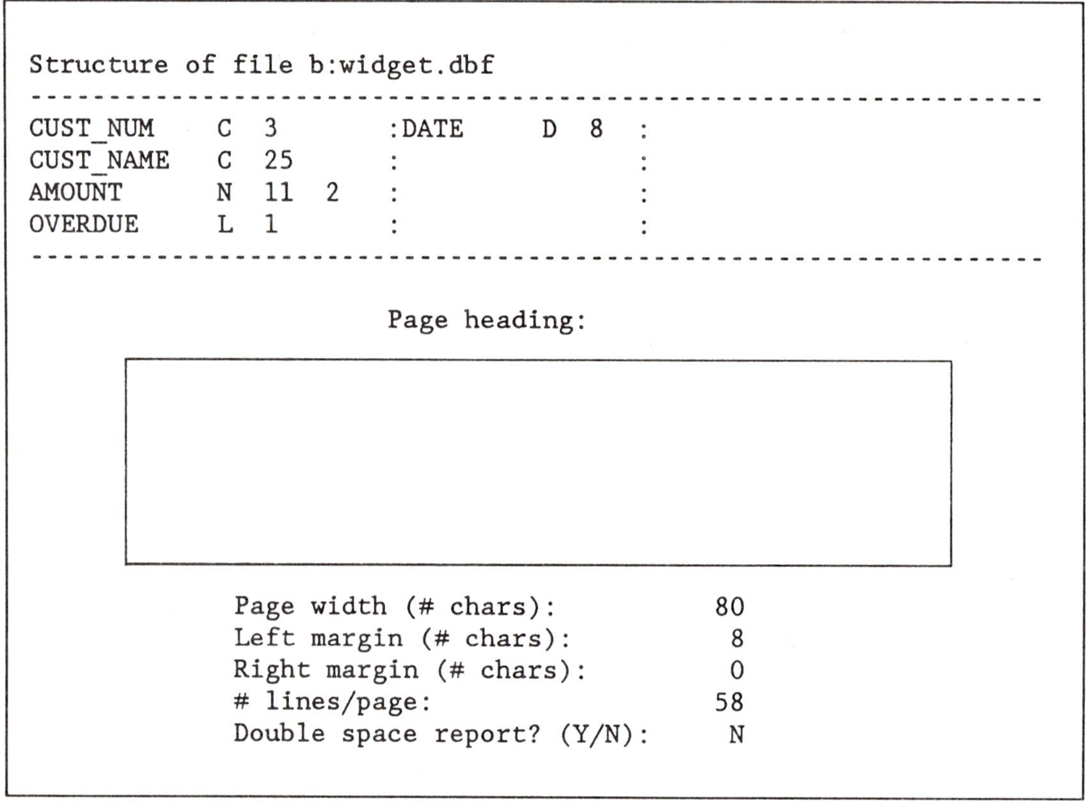

Figure 4.11. Report Questionnaire.

8.   Enter: **Accounts Receivable List By Name**   {**press ENTER key**}

[You have entered the first line of headings for the report.]

9.   Press: **ENTER key four times**

[You have pressed the ENTER key four times to skip over the next three heading lines and to skip over the page width prompt. The cursor should be resting on the left margin question.]

10. Enter: **0**   {press ENTER key}

[You have changed the left margin from 8 characters to 0 characters.]

11. Press: **PGDN key**

[You have pressed the PGDN key to move to the next page of the report questionnaire.]

12. Press: **PGDN key**

[You have pressed the PGDN key to skip the next page on the report questionnaire. The page that is skipped is the subtotals page. Your screen should match figure 4.12.]

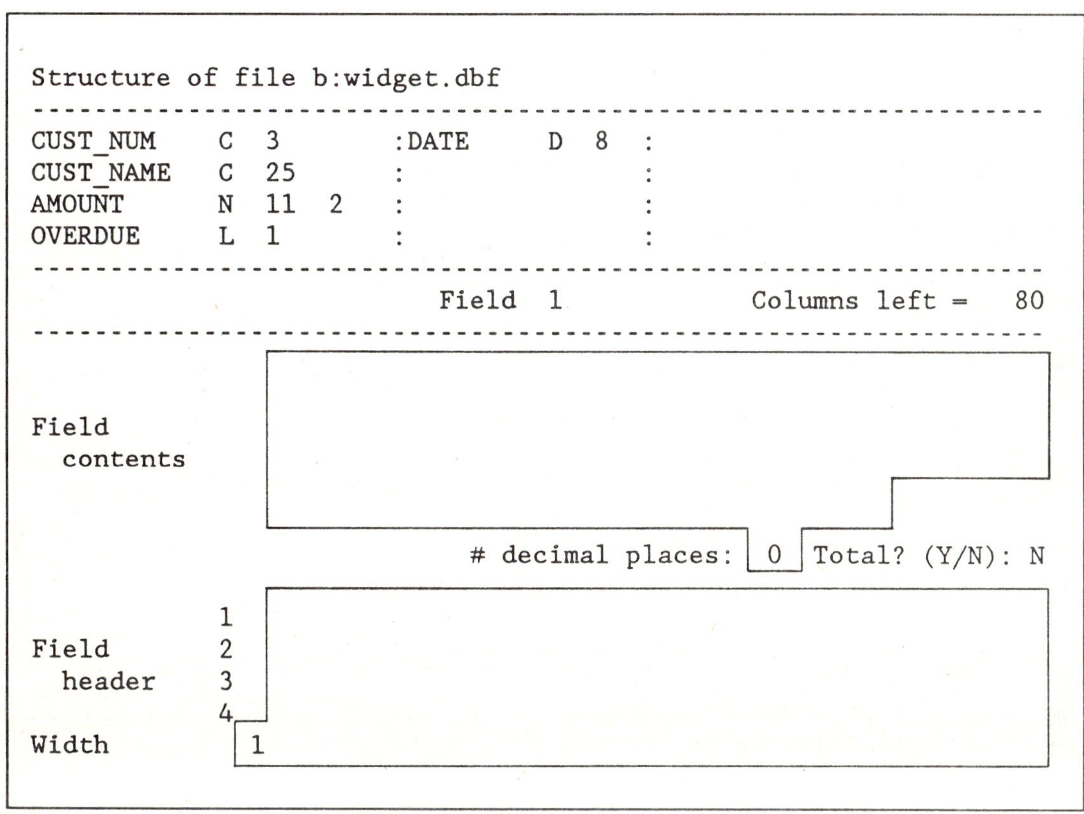

Figure 4.12. Page 2 of the Report Questionnaire.

Fields

1. Enter: **cust_num**   {press ENTER key}

[You have entered the Customer Number field as the field contents of the first field on the report. dBASE III advances the cursor to the field header area.]

2. Enter: **Cust #**   {press ENTER key}

[You have entered Cust # as the first field header on the report.]

3. Press: **PGDN**

[You have pressed the PGDN key to advance to the next field definition screen. Your screen should match figure 4.13.]

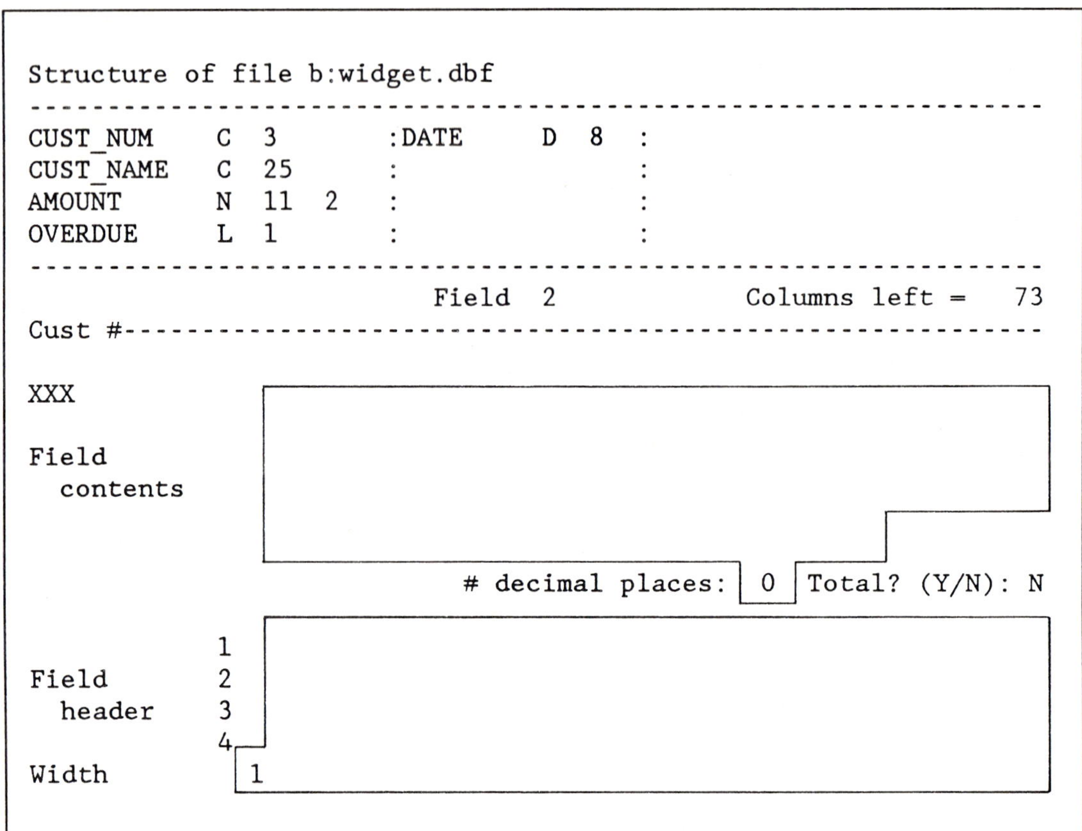

Figure 4.13. The Third Field Definition Screen.

[Note the Cust # "XXX" in the middle of the screen. dBASE III displays the report form field by field as you construct the report. The "XXX" indicates that the cust_num field occupies three positions on the report.]

4. Enter: **cust_name**   {press **ENTER** key}

[You have entered the Customer Name field as the field contents of the second field on the report. dBASE III advances the cursor to the field header area.]

5. Enter: **Customer**   {press **ENTER** key}

[You have entered "Customer" as the first part of a two-part field header.]

6. Enter: **Name**   {press **ENTER** key}

[You have entered "Name" as the second part of a two part field header.]

7. Press: **PGDN**

[You have pressed PGDN to advance to the next field definition screen. Your screen should match figure 4.14.]

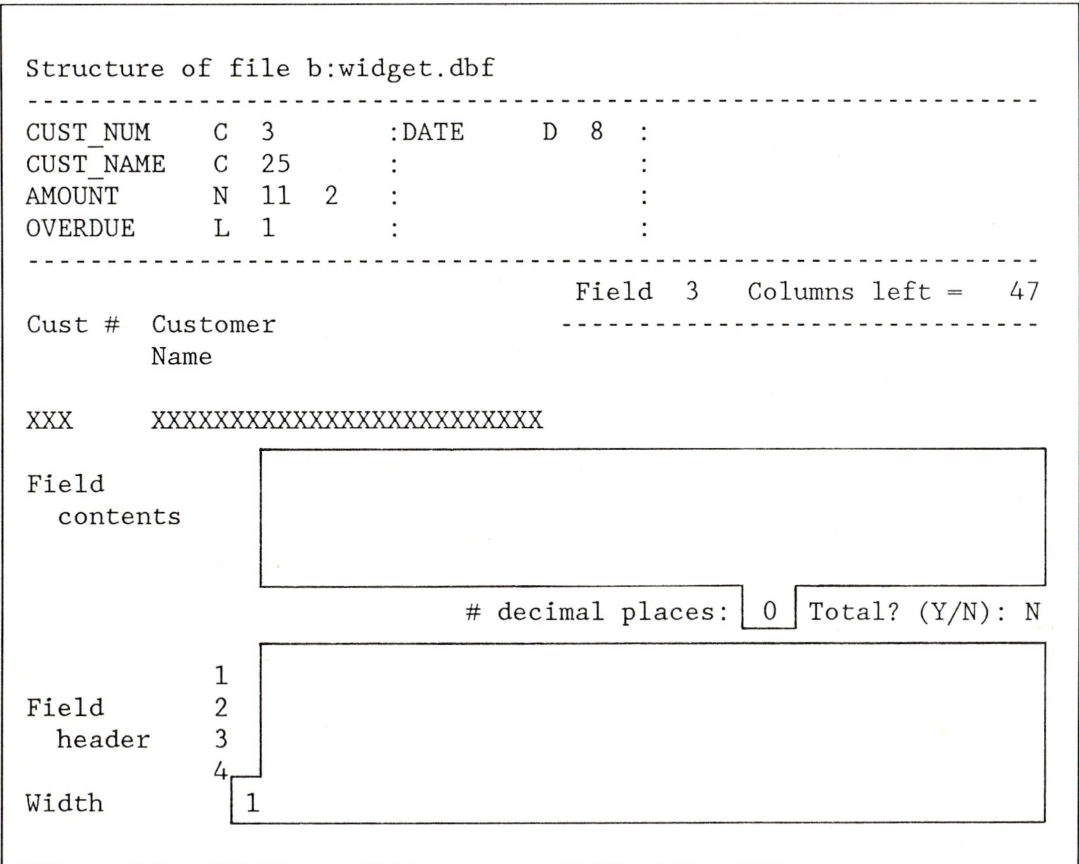

Figure 4.14. The Fourth Field Definition Screen.

8. Enter: **amount**   {press ENTER key}

[You have entered the Amount field as the field contents of the third field on the report.]

9. Press: **ENTER key**

[You have pressed the ENTER key to accept the default of two decimal places for the Amount field.]

10. Enter: **y**

[You enter "Y" to indicate to dBASE III that you wish to total the Amount field on the report. dBASE III advances you to the field header area.]

11. Enter: **Amount**   {press ENTER key}

[You have entered "Amount" as the field header for the Amount field.]

12.   Press: **PGDN**

[You have pressed the PGDN key to advance to the next page of the report definition. Your screen should match figure 4.15.]

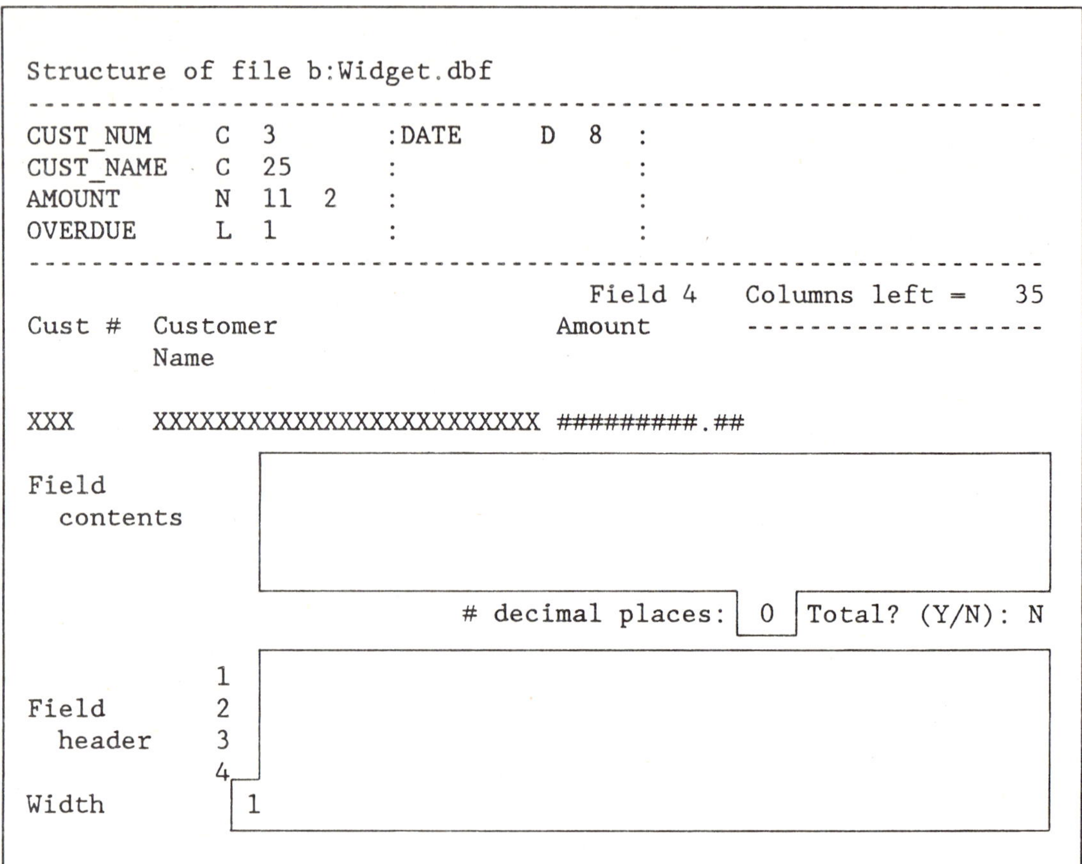

```
Structure of file b:Widget.dbf
---------------------------------------------------------------
CUST_NUM     C   3         :DATE      D   8  :
CUST_NAME  · C   25        :                 :
AMOUNT       N   11  2     :                 :
OVERDUE      L   1         :                 :
---------------------------------------------------------------
                                      Field 4    Columns left =    35
Cust #    Customer                    Amount     ------------------
          Name

XXX       XXXXXXXXXXXXXXXXXXXXXXXXX  #########.##

Field
  contents


                          # decimal places:│ 0 │Total? (Y/N): N

          1
Field     2
  header  3
          4
Width        1
```

Figure 4.15. The Fifth Field Definition Screen.

13.   Enter: **overdue**   {press **ENTER** key}

[You have entered "overdue" as the contents of the fourth field on the report. dBASE III advances you to the field header area.]

14.   Enter: **Overdue**   {press **ENTER** key}

[You have entered "Overdue" as the header for the Overdue field.]

15.   Press: **PGDN**

[You have pressed the PGDN key to advance to the next page of the report definition. Your screen should match figure 4.16.]

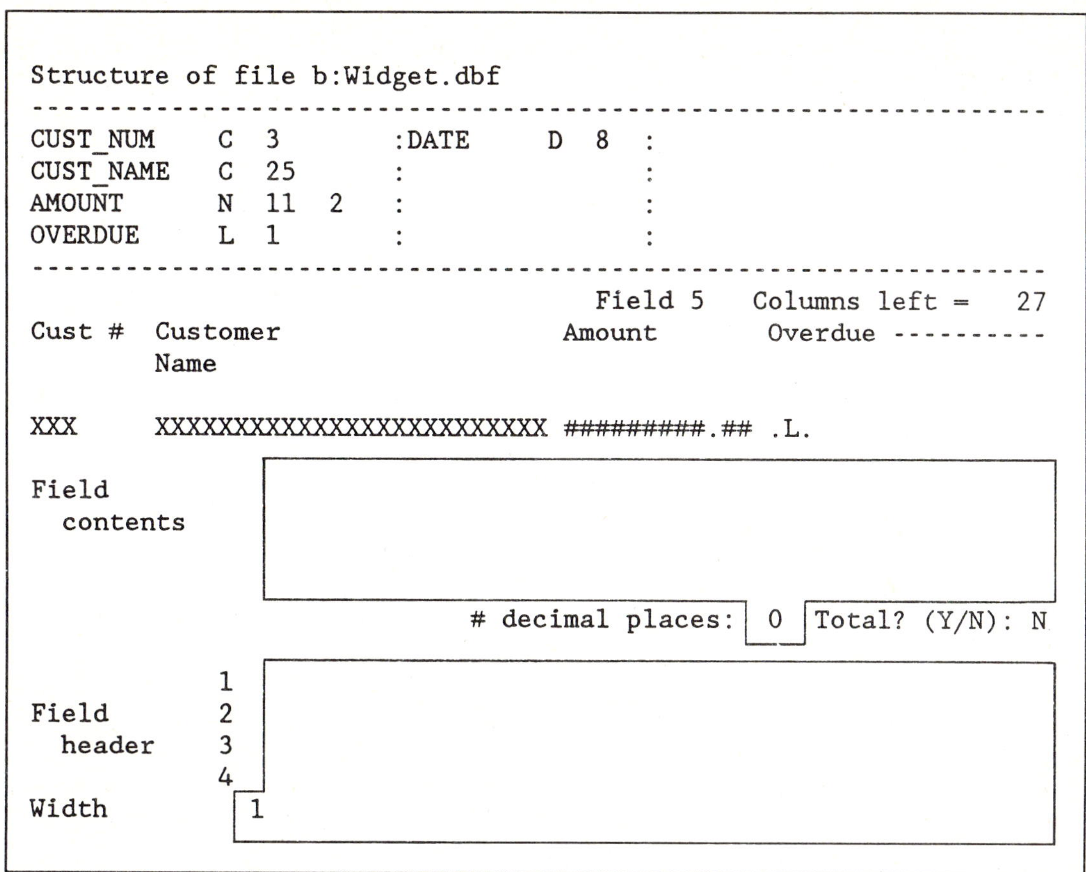

Figure 4.16. The Sixth Field Definition Screen.

16. Press: ^END

[You have pressed ^END to end report creation. The report is saved on disk, and you are returned to the dot prompt.]

View the Report on the Screen

1. Enter: **report form acctlist**   {press ENTER key}

[The report is displayed on the screen. Note that the report is in order by customer name. Your report should match figure 4.17.]

2. Enter: **clear**   {press ENTER key}

3. Enter: **index on amount to widamt**   {press ENTER key}

4. dBASE III displays the following prompt:

WIDAMT.NDX ALREADY EXISTS, OVERWRITE? (Y/N)

```
Page No.       1
07/27/86
                          Accounts Receivable List by name

Cust # Customer                           Amount Overdue
       Name


2        Al Capone Enterprises            75000.00 .T.
4        Bullwinkle Inc.                  78000.00 .T.
1        Deloren Corporation               9000.00 .F.
5        Gumby Ltd.                       35000.00 .F.
3        Sidereal Systems                 28000.00 .F.
*** Total ***

                                         225000.00
```

Figure 4.17. Viewing the Report on the Screen.

5. Enter: **y**

[You enter "Y" to overwrite the old index file.]

6. Enter: **clear**   {press **ENTER key**}

7. Enter: **report form acctlist**   {press **ENTER key**}

[Report is displayed on the screen. Report is now in order by amount. Your report should match figure 4.18.]

```
Page No.       1
07/27/86
                          Accounts Receivable List by name

Cust # Customer                           Amount Overdue
       Name


1        Deloren Corporation               9000.00 .F.
3        Sidereal Systems                 28000.00 .F.
5        Gumby Ltd.                       35000.00 .F.
2        Al Capone Enterprises            75000.00 .T.
4        Bullwinkle Inc.                  78000.00 .T.
*** Total ***

                                         225000.00
```

Figure 4.18. Report Displayed in Order by Amount.

8. Enter: **clear**   {press ENTER key}

Report Form For

You can use the Report Form For command to selectively display only certain records on your report. For example, you are going to use the Report Form For command to only display those records that are overdue. You may use the Report Form For command to report on any subset of your database.

1. Enter: **report form acctlist for overdue**   {press ENTER key}

    [A report is displayed listing only those accounts that are overdue—two accounts are listed. Your report should match figure 4.19.]

```
Page No.      1
07/27/86
                        Accounts Receivable List by name

Cust # Customer                         Amount Overdue
       Name


2       Al Capone Enterprises           75000.00 .T.
4       Bullwinkle Inc.                 78000.00 .T.
*** Total ***

                                       153000.00
```

Figure 4.19. Listing of Overdue Accounts.

2. Enter: **clear**   {press ENTER key}

3. Enter: **report form acctlist for .not. overdue**

4. Press: **ENTER key**

    [A report is displayed listing only those accounts that are not overdue accounts. Three accounts are listed. Your screen should match figure 4.20.]

5. Enter: **clear**   {press ENTER key}

Report Form to Print

So far you have only displayed your reports on the screen. If you have access to a printer, you may also make hardcopy printouts. All you have to do is add the command tail "To Print" to any of your Report Form commands. You must be connected to a printer to use these commands. If you use the To Print option when you are not connected to a printer you will lock up the IBM PC, and you will have to do a "warm boot." You may destroy your database by locking up the system.

```
Page No.       1
07/27/86
                        Accounts Receivable List by name

Cust # Customer                          Amount Overdue
       Name


1         Deloren Corporation            9000.00 .F.
3         Sidereal Systems              28000.00 .F.
5         Gumby Ltd.                    35000.00 .F.
*** Total ***

                                        72000.00
```

Figure 4.20. Listing Accounts Not Overdue.

1. **Move to a PC with a printer to do the following steps.**

2. Enter: **report form acctlist to print**   {press ENTER key}

[The report should match figure 4.21.]

```
Page No.       1
07/27/86
                        Accounts Receivable List by name

Cust # Customer                          Amount Overdue
       Name


1         Deloren Corporation            9000.00 .F.
3         Sidereal Systems              28000.00 .F.
5         Gumby Ltd.                    35000.00 .F.
2         Al Capone Enterprises         75000.00 .T.
4         Bullwinkle Inc.               78000.00 .T.
*** Total ***

                                       225000.00
```

Figure 4.21. Report Form to go to the Printer.

3. Enter: **report form acctlist for overdue to print**

4. Press: **ENTER key**

[Just the overdue accounts will be printed. Your output should match figure 4.22.]

```
Page No.      1
07/27/86
                           Accounts Receivable List by name

Cust # Customer                        Amount Overdue
       Name


2       Al Capone Enterprises          75000.00 .T.
4       Bullwinkle Inc.                78000.00 .T.
*** Total ***
                                      153000.00
```

Figure 4.22. Printout of Overdue Accounts.

Leaving dBASE III

1. Enter: **quit**   {press ENTER key}

[Your screen should match figure 4.23.]

```
 .quit
*** END RUN dBase III
A>
```

Figure 4.23. Leaving dBASE III.

Average	This command is used to compute an arithmetic mean for a numeric field in your database.
Count	This command is used to count the number of any numeric fields within your database.
Display Structure	This command will display a screen that indicates names, field types and field widths of all the fields in your database.
Modify Report	This command is used to create a report and save that report on disk. The command may also be used to change an existing report.
Modify Structure	This command is used to add or delete fields to a database.
Report Form	This command is used to display a report on the screen.
Report Form For	This command is used to selectively display records in a report.
Report Form to Print	This command is used to print a report.
Set Bell Off	Turns the data entry bell off.
Sum	This command is used to sum a numeric field in your database.

_____ 1. This command is used to display a report on the screen.
      a. Recall   b. Report Form   c. Modify Report

_____ 2. This command is used to create a report.
      a. Recall   b. Report Form   c. Modify Report

_____ 3. This command is used to print a report.
      a. Print   b. Display   c. Report Form to Print

_____ 4. This command is used to selectively display records in a report.
      a. Locate For   b. List For   c. Report Form For

_____ 5. This command is used to total a field.
      a. Average   b. Count   c. Sum

_____ 6. This command is used to display the number of items in a particular database.
      a. Average   b. Count   c. Sum

_____ 7. This command is used to take the mean of a field.
      a. Average   b. Count   c. Sum

_____ 8. This command is used to selectively display information in a report.
      a. Report Form For .Not.   b. Average For   c. List For

_____ 9. This command is used to indicate the number of records that match a specific criteria.
      a. Locate For   b. Sum For   c. Count For

_____ 10. This command is used to generate a total for records that match a specific criteria.
      a. Locate For   b. Sum For   c. Count For

1. What command allows you to add new fields to a database. Why would you want to add new fields to a database? How else may this command be used?

2. You have now been introduced to two Set . . . . On/Off commands. Indicate the two commands and indicate when you would use each of the commands.

3. Do you have to include all the fields in your database in a report?

4. Indicate techniques you could use to select which records appear in a report.

5. Indicate the three numeric manipulation commands and explain how each of the commands would be used.

1. Use the file database.

2. Use the Set command to turn the menu on .

3. Use the modify structure command to make the following changes to the file:

    a. Increase the size of the Cust_Name field to 30 positions.

    b. Add a field called Amount. This field should be a numeric field. The Amount field should be 11 characters in width and have 2 decimal positions. The Amount field should be added right after the Cust_Name field. You will use a ^N to add the field.

4. Use the Display Structure command to display the new structure of the database. Enter: display structure and press the ENTER key.

5. Your display should match the following:

```
- - - - - - - - - - - - - - - - - - - - - - - - - - - - - - - - - - - - - - - - - - - - - - - - - - - - - - - - - - - - -
. display structure
Structure for database : B:database.dbf
Number of data records :        2
Date of last update    : 12/24/86
Field    Field name    Type         Width        Dec
   1     CUST_NUM      Character        3
   2     CUST_NAME     Character       30
   3     AMOUNT        Numeric         11           2
   4     STREET        Character       20
   5     CITY          Character       15
   6     STATE         Character        2
   7     ZIP           Character        5
** Total **                           87
- - - - - - - - - - - - - - - - - - - - - - - - - - - - - - - - - - - - - - - - - - - - - - - - - - - - - - - - - - - - -
```

6. Use the append command to add this record {again!!}

```
Customer number: 3
Name: Jones, Spike
Amount: 25000
Street: 11 Loretta Lane
City: Pitsville
State: PA
Zip: 90000
```

7. Use the edit command to add the amounts for the first two records:

```
Customer Number: 1
Name: Hobbs, Calvin B.
Amount: 30000

Customer Number: 2
Name: Drabble, Norman B.
Amount: 50000
```

8. Use the Modify Report command to create a report called report

9. The Report Heading is:

    ```
    Cool Corporation

    Accounts Receivable
    ```

10. The fields used in the report are:

    ```
    Cust_num
    Cust_name
    Amount
    ```

11. The field headings are:

    ```
    Customer Number
    Customer Name
    Amount
    ```

12. The amount field should be totaled.

13. Use the Report Form command to display your report. Your display should match the following:

```
------------------------------------------------------------------------------
        Page No.        1
        12/24/86
                                        Cool Corporation

                                      Accounts Receivable

        Customer Number      Customer Name                           Amount


            1                Hobbs, Calvin B.                      30000.00
            2                Drabble, Norman B.                    50000.00
            3                Jones, Spike                          25000.00

        *** Total ***                                            105000.00
------------------------------------------------------------------------------
```

14. Use the Report Form to Print command to print out the report.

15. Turn in this printout.

<h1 align="center">Appendix A</h1>

<h1 align="center">dBASE III Command Summary</h1>

Append	This command allows information to be added to the active database file using interactive editing on the screen.
Assist	Calls dBASE assistant.
Average	This command is used to compute an arithmetic mean for a numeric field in your database.
Browse	This command allows full screen viewing and modification of multiple records on all or selected fields.
Clear	This command clears the screen.
Copy	This command allows part of or all of the current database file to be copied to another file.
Count	This command is used to count the number of any numeric fields within your database.
Create	This command is used to produce a new database file. It lets you define the structure of database records and, optionally, start entering information.
dBASE	Starts dBASE III program.
Delete	This command allows records to be marked for deletion, but does not actually remove them.
Delete For	This command allows you to mark for deletion records that match a particular criteria.
Display	This command shows requested information from the active database file. You can specify which records should be shown and what information within the records to include.
Display All	This command displays all the records in the database with all the fields.
Display For	This command displays the records that match a particular criteria.
Display Record #	This command displays one particular record.
Display Structure	This command will display a screen that indicates the field names, field types and field widths of all the fields in your database.

Edit	This command allows interactive editing of a single record on the screen. The current record is assumed.
Erase	This command is used to delete a file.
Index	This command is a faster way to order records than the Sort command.
Locate	This command is used to find data records.
Modify Report	This command is used to create a report and save that report on disk. The command may also be used to change an existing report.
Modify Structure	This command is used to add or delete fields to a database.
Quit	This command exits dBASE III and returns to DOS.
Recall	This command is used to reactivate records that are marked for deletion. This command will work on the entire database unless a limiting condition is given.
Recall All	This command allows you to unmark all records that are marked for deletion.
Report Form	This command is used to display a report on the screen.
Report Form For	This command is used to selectively display records in a report.
Report Form to Print	This command is used to print a report.
Set Bell Off	Turns the data entry bell off.
Set Menu On	Turns the Data Entry, Edit, and Browse menus on.
Sort	This command allows you to sequence a database file in either ascending or descending order on one or more fields.
Sum	This command is used to sum a numeric field in your database.
Use	Allows you to select the active or working database file from existing database files, and optionally, an index file.
^End	Command to exit a dBASE function.

Appendix B
Assist Menu Summary

—Assistant Main Menu—

—dBASE III Assistant—

Set Up	Modify	Position	Retrieve	Organize	Utilities

The Assistant Main Menu is the gateway menu to all other menus in the Assist system.

—Modify Database Menu—

—Modify Database—

Append	Browse	Edit	Delete	Recall	Replace	Position

The Modify menu allows you to view, change, and remove information in the active database file. You may work with a single record or multiple records using either interactive editing on the screen or command driven editing.

—Organize Database Menu—

—Organize Database—

Index	Sort	Copy	Pack

This menu is used to create indexes for fast key searches, sort a database file by field contents, copy a database file, and remove information marked for deletion.

–Retrieve and Present Information–

Display	Sum	Average	Count	Label	Report	Position

The Retrieve menu provides several ways to view and summarize information. You may view single or multiple records in raw form or in report format. Summary information is available as simple totals or through subtotals in reports.

–Set Up Environment Menu–

–Set Up Environment–

Use	Set Drive	Create	Create Label	Create Report

The Set Up menu allows you to establish the active database file either by creating a new one or by selecting an existing one. It also lets you create label and report layouts. Other menu options are inactive until an active database is available.

dBASE III Glossary

Active Database	Only one database can be in use at one time. The database that is in use is called the active database.
Character Field	A dBASE III field that may contain any character in the character set.
Data	Information that you store in your database file.
Database files (.dbf)	The file that contains your records and fields.
Database Structure	The field names, field types, and field lengths that make up your database.
Date Field	A dBASE III field that contains a date in the mm/dd/yy format.
Default Menu Choice	The first menu choice in each Assist menu.
Dot Prompt	This is the prompt displayed by dBASE III. It tells you that dBASE III is ready for your next command.
Field	A group of consecutive characters that contain data on one item.
File	A group of records makes up a file.
Form Files (.fmt)	These are the report layout files created by the Modify Report command.
Index Files (.ndx)	The files that contain the record number and the index field or fields used to order your data.
Logical Field	A dBASE III field that contains a value of "True" or "False."
Menu Cursor	An inverse bar that highlights a menu item.
Numeric Field	A dBASE III field that can only contain numbers, decimal points, and a plus or a minus sign.
Record	A group of fields makes up a record.
Sort	Describes the process of ordering a database file into some logical sequence.